street food

from around
the world

street food
from around
the world

JAMES MAYSON

Absolute Press

STREET FOOD FROM AROUND THE WORLD

**This United Kingdom edition published in 2003 by
Absolute Press, Scarborough House, 29 James Street West,
Bath, BA1 2BT, England.
First published in the United Kingdom in 1998.**

First published in Australasia in 1997 by
Simon & Schuster Australia
20 Barcoo Street, East Roseville NSW 2069

A Viacom Company
Sydney   New York   London   Toronto   Tokyo   Singapore

Text and travel photography © James Mayson 1997

ISBN 1 899791 81 7

Art direction by Jacqui Trigg
Cover photograph by James Mayson
Photography by Craig Cranko
Styling by Philippa Wight
Food by James Mayson

Printed by Butler and Tanner, Frome, England.

contents

From the chaotic bazaars of southern India and the serenity of the Nepalese Himalaya to the steaming jungles of Sumatra and the cobbled labyrinths of Mexico City — wherever marketplace cooks and street-side vendors hold court, great food is but one of the many pleasures to enjoy.

Feasting on fresh regional fare from the comfort of a rickety bench, it's almost impossible not to be swept up in the visual panorama of everyday life bustling by. There's local gossip going on all around, jokes being shared, business deals being thrashed out and romantic interludes to observe. The roadside caterer has a multitude of roles to perform — confidant, shrink and storyteller, doctor, noticeboard and prophet. These original fast-food operators may have ideologies and temperaments as varied as their mouthwatering morsels, yet they share one thing in common: a lack of arrogance in their approach — after all, they are essentially 'people pleasers'.

Street food is the ultimate 'snack' food. Although the execution may at times seem unsophisticated, defying strict adherence to old cooking-school rules, the results are in fact a product of hundreds of years of refinement. Yet there are no hard and fast rules, and most dishes continue to be reworked according to the size of the cook's pinch, the availability of fresh produce and the demanding whims of patrons. Street food is also extremely versatile — whether you wish to compile a menu from around the globe or just sample a quick 'fix', the flexibility and, in most cases, one-pot execution makes it accessible no matter how advanced your skills.

As an avid traveller whose budget is best described as shoestring, I could hardly exist without the efforts of the street-side vendor. In many countries they provide the most economic form of nourishment as well as allowing for invaluable contact with the locals. Food, after all, is about *people*. It is inseparable from the social makeup of a country, its geography, climate and religion, its history and its future. What could be more crucial to the existence of a culture than the food that has sustained it?

Wandering through a bustling market, absorbing the sights, sounds and aromas, sampling all that is on offer (too often allowing my curiosity to get the better of me!) and, of course, interacting with the farmers, artisans, butchers and fruit and vegetable vendors is, to me, the true essence of travel.   Nowhere is this more applicable than in a country's national celebrations, where food is often the guest of honour. Song, dance and prayer are all part of the tribute to ensure or give thanks for a bountiful harvest. Tools are crafted to till and reap, pots and utensils used to cook and eat with, and ceramics and baskets to serve and display. Food is also at the very core of all traditional medicine, responsible for the health of families, communities and, indeed, entire nations. Food is the great unifier — bringing together the family, the village and the culture.

Street Food has been compiled over the past eight years of my global meanderings. It is a personal 'snapshot' and is in no way meant as a formative guide. Primarily, it is a collection of the reknowned and the unusual dishes that I relished while backpacking around the world. *Street Food* is a nostalgic embrace of some truly great times and an attempt to recreate not only the fare but also the festivity — to transport the reader, to savour the circumstance, meet the eccentric characters and evoke some of the ambience. In most cases these recipes were absorbed from hours of observation and furious note-taking, others were gladly passed on with explicit instructions, and the remainder grafted by pitting my memory against trial and error. The starting point was authenticity, and the central aim to keep to the integrity of the original as much as possible. It is also my wish to pay homage to the foundations of international cuisine while encouraging experimentation — just as with any street hawker who leaves the condiments and sauces for the individual palate to complete — the idea is to indulge your fancies.

Enjoy!

indonesia

Blessed with a multitude
of influences from inter-island migration
and steeped in the history of colonial conquest
and trade, Indonesia has one of the most diverse cuisines
in the world. If variety is the spice of life,
then these are the islands that harbour
the aromas of diversity.

From the last outposts of the British and Dutch empires, through the fiercely independent tribes of northern Sumatra, the Muslim crush of Java, the Hindu descendants of Bali, and out to the Christian enclave of Flores, Indonesia continues to juggle the most disparate group of islands in an effort to forge its own identity.

Indonesia is the largest country in Southeast Asia, a meandering archi-pelago of nearly 14,000 islands. Although spread out over a large area, Indonesia straddles the equator and the climate is distinctly tropical, but it's the diversity of the people in each region that creates such a wide range of food styles. The religious background and ancestral heritage of many regions varies to such an extent that Indonesia seems less of a nation than a loose federation of autonomous states. While the government and, more importantly the military, views this diversity in terms of control and assimilation, many of the islands remain defiantly independent, and it is this variety that makes Indonesia such a fascinating point of focus when it comes to street food.

My introduction to Indonesia came via a serpentine bus journey that cut across northern Sumatra – a bone-rattling wake-up call to the savage nature of the landscape – so large are the plants and so wild the sky that it's easy to imagine one is travelling through the land that time forgot. The journey can be broken in several places, but the visual magnificence of two stops in particular, the Caldera Lakes of Toba and Maninjau, are etched into my memory – like colossal baths for the gods, brimming with the reflections of the giant sky.

On reaching West Sumatra, we came across the first of many 'cuisines'. Padang is the capital of the province and is famous for a style of food that bears the city's name. Despite the fact that meals are almost exclusively eaten cold, the heat of the spices imparts the most intense flavours. Everything is displayed and ordered from large bowls that sit in glass cabinets either at the front of the restaurant or, in the case of street vendors, on battle-scarred tin plates.

On a lopsided ferry we lurched towards the main island of Java and another world entirely. Jakarta is a city in a cyclone, flailing itself in a desperate bid to catch up with the modern world and shedding its traditional way of life in the wake of a massive industrial and technological transformation. Street stalls are disappearing beneath the golden arches of western-style fast food chains and lackadaisical markets are becoming a thing of the past. However to the east lies the cultural heartland of Java: Yogyakarta. A city of bicycle rickshaws, batik and labyrinthine avenues crammed with Indonesian street stalls – the *warungs*. Nearby are two of the most remarkable historical sites on the entire archipelago, if not the world: Borobudur and Prambanan. Borobodor, a breath-taking monument to the piety of humankind, is the single largest Buddhist monument in the world and, along with Angkor Wat in Cambodia, Southeast Asia's most distinguished site. It is framed like a precious stone, set amongst towering palms, green velvet rice paddies and the distinct backdrop of a volcanic mountain range. After assailing the nine levels – symbolic of humanity's transition from earth-bound creature to one free of the chains of desire – one realises that one is not alone, for at the top is a series of life-sized buddhas in reflective repose. A truly humbling experience.

The Hindu temple complex of Prambanan conjures up a completely different aura. As luck would have it, my visit coincided with a performance of the Ramayana Ballet – a mythical tale originating in India that has been endowed with the unmistakable costumes and dance of the Javanese. Yogyakarta is also known for the *wayang kulit* (shadow puppet plays) that are a combination of Indian fable, animist symbolism and Indonesian subjectivity, backed by a percussional orchestra – *gamelan* – that is unique to the country. Within the music there is order, melody and nuance (so I am informed!), but it *sounds* like a fantastic excursion to the outskirts of the avant-garde. Needless to say that along with all this frenetic, cross-cultural influence, comes the fusion of cuisines. Most prominent of these is Indian, which is reflected in the nation's tendency towards food rich in spice and bold of flavour. In particular, the piquancy from the south of India, with which Indonesia shares a similar climate, and the bountiful seafood and ever-present coconut. No surprise then that Indonesia has also inherited rice as their staple food, although on some of the more isolated islands, the traditional staples such as cassâva, corn and potatoes still prevail. Turmeric, ground coriander, cumin, fenugreek, garlic, ginger and tamarind are all reminiscent of the spices from southern India. Such is Indonesia's own ability to transform outside influences that the street food presiding on the roadsides today bears little resemblance to traditional Indian cuisine.

One of the idiosyncracies of Indonesia is that amongst its broad band of cultures, it boasts the largest Muslim population in the world. Although the form of Islam practised is less strict than in the Middle East, there is a strong affinity with the universal suffering of their Islamic brothers. This, naturally, has a huge effect on the types of food eaten in Indonesia. Yet, while the majority of the population refrains from eating pork, the very north of Sumatra, North Sulawesi and Bali are famous for their pork dishes.

Bali, in particular, with its vibrant mix of animism and Hinduism, has a cuisine that combines the rich spice of the region with a devout and sophisticated culture to create a culinary artform worthy of its own chapter in this book. The Balinese are the undisputed experts when it comes to the spit barbecue. Here, more than anywhere else on the archipelago, food is an inseparable part of religious celebrations. Weddings are occasions of sumptuous feasts with the meal forming just part of an ornate decoration. The dishes are presented on beds of banana leaves and palm fronds, surrounded by a kaleidoscope of flowers, including fragrant orchids, and carved fruit.

The Balinese are also artisans par excellence. In stonework, woodwork, painting, dance and music, their aesthetic sense and raw creativity make this tiny island a cultural wonderland.

The close proximity of Indonesian's Asian neighbours, in particular Malaysia, with whom they share a common language, brings together still more influences, while a trail of ingredients that includes shrimp paste, ginger, lemon grass, kaffir lime leaves and galangal can be traced all the way north to Thailand.

Southeast Asia's largest migrant community, the Chinese, have brought their own cooking methods and flavours which have been converted into two of Indonesia's perennial favourites, **mie goreng** (fried noodles) and **nasi goreng** (fried rice). *Soto ayam*, a chicken noodle soup very similar to Chinese *ramen*, is extremely popular, as is the imaginative use of one of China's great gifts to the region, tofu. Finally, there is the absolute *warung* champion, *campur goreng*, or simply *campur*, a rough translation is 'mix', though a

closer approximation would be plain rice topped with … well… whatever's leftover.

As opposed to the influence of immigration, the grip of empire – in particular the Dutch – has gradually lost its sway. At the peak of Dutch trading power, Indonesia was their goldmine, or to be more precise, spice mine. Like all colonialists they had the locals devise food that was agreeable to their palate. One such dish that still bears their mark is **pergredel jagung** or corn fritters. *Rijstafel* is another, a sort of festive gourmet smorgasbord devised to grace the tables of the landed gentry. With saffron rice, various curries, chutneys, seafood, meat, eggs, fruit and nuts, it is hardly street food but is worth a mention for its sheer decadence.

Indonesia has not taken on these influences without doing a little adjusting of its own. The soy sauce used in almost every dish is quite different from that which originated in China. The most common form known as *kecap manis* – literally, sweet ketchup – resembles a thick syrup fortified with corn starch and sugar, and is excellent in stir-fries and sauces. *Sambal olek* is pure dynamite – fresh crushed chillies, sometimes mixed with garlic and spices, preserved in vinegar – and frequently abused to put spark in many dishes. From this comes what the Indonesians loosely term **sambal kecap** – a kind of homemade, go-with-anything cooked salsa that has as many variations a there are islands. The ubiquitous peanut, fried, crushed, and cooked with coconut cream, is almost synonymous with Indonesian cuisine, especially in the much imitated versions of **saté** and **gado gado**, while the highly acquired taste of *tempeh* – a fermented soy bean 'cake' – is thrown about with abandon in stir-fries or as a snack on its own.

Indonesia's confetti of islands provides rich pickings – it almost goes without saying that seafood is predominant everywhere. Even in modest homes, fish is a common addition to the main meal, while prawns and squid are popular items at many street-side stalls. Fertile volcanic soil and a tropical climate compliment the oceans, bearing on immense variety of fruit and vegetables.

With regional and religious variations that have evolved from such a diversity of peoples, it is not hard to see why Indonesia is one of the most dynamic and varied contributors to the culture of street food.

1kg (2lb) lamb, cut into
10cm x 2cm
(4in x $^3/_4$in) strips
24 wooden skewers,
soaked in water for
2 hours

MARINADE
4 cloves garlic, crushed
5cm (2in) piece ginger,
finely chopped
1 tsp sambal olek or 2
red chillies, finely
chopped
1 cup tamarind water
(see glossary)
1 tbsp peanut oil
2 tbsp kecap manis
(see glossary)
1 tsp ground coriander
salt and freshly ground
black pepper

SATÉ KAMBING
[lamb satay]

The aroma of the ultimate snack!
All over Indonesia, just as dusk begins to devour the last rays of the
sun, the satay vendors are bent over their charcoal fires,
fanning the coals with banana leaves and broadcasting their wares
to muster the hungry.

combine the marinade ingredients in a ceramic or glass bowl. Add the lamb strips and toss until well coated. leave to marinate in the refrigerator for at least 2 hours.

thread the strips of lamb onto wooden skewers and barbecue over glowing coals for 3–5 minutes, basting frequently with the remaining marinade.

serve with plain white rice and **bumbu saté**.

[**note:** other meats can also be used — chicken is particularly good when a teaspoon of ground turmeric is added to the marinade. pay close attention to cooking time, especially with chicken as it has a tendency to dry out.]

BUMBU SATÉ
[satay sauce]

An all purpose peanut satay sauce that's great to serve as an
accompaniment to any grilled meats.

fry the onion, garlic, ginger, shrimp paste and brown sugar in the vegetable oil for 5 minutes. stir in the peanuts until well coated, then pour in the coconut cream and simmer for 15 minutes. stir in the lemon juice, *kecap manis* and chillies and season with salt and pepper.

to serve, pour over satay skewers and garnish with spring onion.

Makes about 2 cups

1 onion, diced
2 cloves garlic, chopped
2 knobs ginger, chopped
$1/2$ tsp shrimp paste
(see glossary)
1 tsp brown sugar
1 tbsp vegetable oil
200g (7oz) peanuts, fried
or roasted, then chopped
2 cups coconut milk
2 tbsp lemon juice
2 tbsp kecap manis
(see glossary)
2 red chillies, finely
chopped
salt and freshly ground
black pepper
1 spring onion (scallion),
sliced

SAMBAL GORENG TELOR
[spiced eggs]

Among the dozens of mysterious dishes that symbolise Padang food,
spiced eggs appear almost welcoming and, to a newly arrived foreigner,
at least recogniseable. The spiciness may seem excessive to some,
but with plenty of plain white rice, it is a very tasty
and fairly effortless dish.

cook the eggs in boiling water for 10 minutes until they are hard-boiled, then immerse in cold water and remove shells.

blend the onion, garlic and spices (except the cardamom pods) in a food processor or blender.

fry the paste in vegetable oil until fragrant, about 2–3 minutes. gradually stir in the coconut milk, add the eggs and the cardamom pods and simmer for 5 minutes.

season to taste with salt and pepper and serve with plenty of white rice.

Serves 5–6

10–12 eggs
1 onion
2 cloves garlic, chopped
2.5cm (1in) piece ginger,
chopped
1 tsp coriander seeds
2 red chillies, chopped
1 tsp ground cumin
1 tsp ground turmeric
$1/2$ tsp ground fenugreek
2 tsp vegetable oil
2 cardamom pods, split
4 cups coconut milk
salt and freshly ground
black pepper

2 tbsp vegetable oil
2 eggs, lightly beaten
200g (7oz) chicken, beef
or pork, cut into small
cubes
1 onion, cut into thin
wedges
1 large carrot, diced
1 red pepper, diced
1 green pepper, diced
2.5cm (1in) ginger, finely
sliced
2 cloves garlic,
finely chopped
1 spring onion
(scallion), sliced
100g (3$^1/_2$ oz) dried
prawns, soaked in hot
water for 15 minutes
and drained
1 tbsp kecap manis
(see glossary)
1 tsp sambal olek
(see glossary)
$^1/_2$ cup tempeh, diced
(see glossary)
$^1/_2$ cup peanuts,
roughly chopped
1 cup bean sprouts
500g (1lb) fresh
Chinese-style hokkein
egg noodles, prepared
according to packet
directions
extra chopped spring
onions (scallions) or
coriander leaves

MIE GORENG
[fried noodles]

Despite the vast differences between regions, beliefs and traditions,
the Indonesians do have culinary symphony of sorts in a
number of dishes. **Mie goreng** *(sometimes known as* bakmie goreng*)*
and **nasi goreng** *are to be found in almost every cluster*
of warungs *across the archipelago. Yet try to track down the recipe*
and you will be laughed at — the nature and indeed
beauty of these dishes is that they're made with whatever is available.
Every stallholder has their secret, which only fueled my curiosity.

drizzle a teaspoon of oil into a large, heavy-based wok over low heat and pour in the eggs, tilting the wok to form a thin omelette. when the bottom has just set, poke a few holes in it to allow any uncooked egg to run through and cook. as soon as all the egg has set, remove to a plate. when cool, cut into 2cm (3/4in) strips.

heat the remaining oil in the wok and stir-fry the meat until just browned. add the onion, carrot and peppers and stir-fry for 2–3 minutes, then add the ginger, garlic, spring onion and prawns. continue to stir-fry for a further 2 minutes. add the *kecap manis* and *sambal olek*, tossing the ingredients quickly to coat with sauce. add the tempeh, peanuts and bean sprouts, and continue to toss for 2 minutes. finally, add the noodles and toss until warmed through, about 1 minute.

remove from heat. serve topped with chopped omelette and garnished with chopped spring onions or coriander leaves.

variation: the noodles can be fried crisp and served as a base underneath the stir-fried ingredients. to make crispy noodles, soak fresh noodles in hot water for 5 minutes; drain well and spread out on tea towels to dry. heat $^1/_2$ cup vegetable oil in a wok until just smoking and add the noodles, separating them as best you can. turn the noodles over and fry on the other side until they are crisp and golden. remove and drain on absorbent paper. when the stir-fry ingredients are cooked, break up the noodles onto serving plates and pour the stir-fry over the top. serve immediately so the noodles remain crisp.

NASI GORENG

[fried rice]

heat half the oil in a heavy-based wok on high and stir-fry the meat until brown on all sides. add the onion, carrots and peppers and stir-fry for 2 minutes. add the ginger, garlic, prawns, tomatoes and spring onion and stir-fry for a further 2 minutes. stir in the pre-cooked rice, making sure that it doesn't stick to the base of the wok — add an extra $1/2$ tablespoon of oil if necessary. stir in the *tempeh* and peanuts, then pour in the *kecap manis* and *sambal olek* and toss so that all the ingredients are coated. stir-fry for a further minute then remove from heat.

in a separate frying pan, heat the remaining vegetable oil and lightly fry the eggs, keeping the yolks intact.

to serve, fill a small bowl with the rice mix and unmould it in the centre of each serving plate. top with a fried egg and garnish with a few coriander leaves.

2 tbsp vegetable oil
200g (7oz) chicken, beef or pork, cut into small cubes
1 onion, diced
1 large carrot, diced
1 red pepper, diced
1 green pepper, diced
2.5cm (1in) piece ginger, finely sliced
2 cloves garlic, finely chopped
100g ($3^1/2$oz) dried shrimp, soaked in hot water for 15 minutes and drained
2 medium tomatoes, diced
1 spring onion (scallion), sliced
4 cups cooked long-grain rice
$1/2$ cup tempeh, diced *TOFU* (see glossary)
1/2 cup peanuts, roughly chopped
1 tbsp kecap manis *SALSA* (see glossary)
1 tsp sambal olek *CHILLI* (see glossary)
4 eggs
coriander leaves

RENDANG DAGING
[rich beef curry]

10 birdseye chillies,
soaked in warm water
for 10 minutes, then
drained
2 onions, chopped
2 cloves garlic, chopped
5cm (2in) piece galangal,
chopped
1 tbsp coriander seeds
1 tbsp cumin seeds
1 tbsp shrimp paste
(see glossary)
1 stalk lemon grass,
white part only, sliced
6 candlenuts
(see glossary)
4 tbsp vegetable oil
1kg (2lb) chuck or blade
steak
4 cups coconut milk,
plus $^1/_2$ cup extra
$^1/_2$ cup tamarind water
(see glossary)
2 kaffir lime leaves
2 tbsp kecap manis
(see glossary)
salt and freshly
ground black pepper

Bahasa, the official language of both Indonesia and Malaysia,
has an endearing and cheeky way of expressing a continuing action
or exaggerating a point: jalan *is walk,* jalan jalan *is walking;*
cumi cumi *is squid, perhaps because of it's many tentacles;*
enak *is 'good taste',* enak enak *is really delicious.*
(I'll leave jiggi jiggi *to your imagination!)* **Rendang,** *as it's often*
shortened to, is the most more-ish of all curries in the region — rich and
spicy, it's the dish that has me stringing together the most enaks.

place the chillies, onions, garlic, galangal, spices, shrimp paste, lemon grass and candlenuts in a food processor or blender and blend to a paste.

heat the vegetable oil in a heavy-based frying pan and fry the paste until fragrant, about 2–3 minutes. add the meat and fry for a further 3 minutes, then pour in the coconut milk and simmer until the beef is tender, about 1 hour. add the remaining ingredients, season to taste with salt and pepper, and continue to simmer until the oil separates from the rich gravy and the curry is almost dry.

serve with plenty of plain white rice.

[**note:** in indonesia, **rendang daging** is often left overnight to allow the flavours to develop, and served cold the next day.]

PERGREDEL JAGUNG
[corn fritters]

A legacy of the Dutch empire? Or a typically Indonesian way of making the most of a meagre cupboard? No matter what their origin, **pergredel jagung** *are a favourite on the sidewalks of Jakarta.*

5 cooked corn cobs
or 500g (1 lb) corn
kernels
2 cloves garlic, chopped
2 red chillies, chopped
1 tbsp ground coriander
$^1/_2$ cup tapioca flour
$^1/_2$ cup coconut milk
2 eggs, beaten
4 spring onions
(scallions), sliced
$^1/_2$ bunch coriander,
leaves and roots, finely
chopped
salt and freshly
ground black pepper
vegetable oil

scrape the corn kernels from the cobs and combine half with the garlic, chillies and ground coriander in a food processor or blender and blend to a paste.

mix the tapioca flour, coconut milk, eggs, spring onions, fresh coriander and the remaining corn kernels in a large bowl. stir in the paste, and season to taste with salt and pepper.

shallow-fry spoonfuls of the mixture in oil until golden brown, turning just once.

drain on paper towels and serve at once with **sambal kecap** (page 12).

Makes about 2 cups

2 tbsp vegetable oil
1 tbsp shrimp paste
(see glossary)
2 onions, diced
4 cloves garlic, crushed
5cm (2in) piece ginger,
finely chopped
10 birdseye chillies,
soaked in warm water
for 10 minutes, then
drained and chopped
2 tsp ground coriander
2 tsp ground cumin
6 medium tomatoes,
chopped
2 spring onions
(scallions), finely sliced
2 tbsp palm sugar
or raw sugar
1 bunch coriander, roots
only, finely chopped
2 tbsp tamarind water
(see glossary)
1 cup water
2 tbsp kecap manis
(see glossary)
juice of 2 limes or
lemons
salt and freshly ground
black pepper

SAMBAL KECAP
[hot chilli sauce]

*This cooked salsa is to be found on just about every street-vendor's
counter. No two are the same, and variations are encouraged.
Many find the chilli content blindingly hot, so don't hesitate to alter
the ingredients to suit your own tastes.
It can be served accompanied by a bowl of plain white rice
and a simple dish of fried fish or chicken, or as an integral
part of an Indonesian banquet.*

in a heavy-based saucepan, warm the vegetable oil over low heat and fry the shrimp paste until fragrant, about 2 minutes. add the onions, garlic, ginger, chillies and spices and cook for a further 2 minutes. add the tomatoes, spring onions, sugar and coriander roots and cook until all the moisture has evaporated. stir in the tamarind water, water and *kecap manis* and reduce until the sauce has a very thick consistency.

remove from heat, stir in the lime or lemon juice, and season to taste with salt and pepper. store in an airtight container in the refrigerator for up to two weeks.

RUJAK
[spicy fruit salad]

This was a huge favourite of mine in the mountain village of
Bukit Tinggi. Every morning I would sit and watch as the warung
owner ground up the bumbu *to order, then served the salad*
on a fresh banana leaf. I would gobble down the fruit
before the chilli began to hit me, then head down to the market,
fired up for yet another lesson in haggling.

to make the *bumbu,* grind the peanuts, shrimp paste, banana, lemon juice, sugar and chillies to a coarse paste in a mortar, or blend in a food processor or blender. thin out with the tamarind water until the paste is the consistency of a very thick sauce — the occasional crunch of peanut adds to the texture. season to taste with salt and pepper.

to assemble the salad, slice the fruit, toss in the *bumbu* and serve.

$^1/_2$ *pawpaw (papaya)*
$^1/_2$ *pineapple*
1 pomelo (see glossary)
or sweet grapefruit
1 cucumber
2 mangoes, slightly
under-ripe
2 bananas
2 granny smith apples

BUMBU
1 cup peanuts,
fried or roasted
1 tsp shrimp paste,
grilled (see glossary)
$^1/_2$ *unripe cooking*
banana, chopped
1 tbsp lemon juice
1 tbsp brown sugar
1–2 red chillies,
chopped,
to taste
1–2 tbsp tamarind water
(see glossary)
salt and freshly ground
black pepper

2 large potatoes, diced
1 large yam, diced
1 cup cauliflower florets
1 cup sliced green beans
1 cup sliced carrot
shredded cabbage or
lettuce
2 tomatoes, quartered
1 cup bean sprouts
1 cucumber, sliced
2 hard-boiled eggs, sliced
bumbu saté (page 7)
4 prawn crackers
coriander leaves,
chopped

GADO GADO
[vegetable salad with peanut sauce]

Perhaps the best known of all Indonesia's dishes, **gado gado** *makes the perfect light lunch. The combination of raw and cooked vegetables with a warm sauce is sublime and can be found, allowing for regional variations, on just about every island in the archipelago.*

steam or boil the potatoes, yam, cauliflower, beans and carrot until just cooked and refresh under cold water to maintain their bright colour.

layer the serving plates with some shredded cabbage or lettuce and mound the vegetables in the centre, alternating layers of cooked and raw ingredients. finish with a few slices of hard-boiled egg. pour over warm **bumbu saté**. garnish with coriander leaves and a prawn cracker.

SAMBAL GORENG UDANG
[prawns with spicy sauce]

Serves 4

On the southern coast of Lombok, I experienced a serene alternative to the tourist-battered Kuta in Bali. Near a beach that was unpopulated but for the small fishing boats putting out to sea each morning, I stayed with a three-generation family whose existence was the very essence of self-sufficiency. A few buffalo, a couple of chickens, a vegetable patch and the morning's catch. This is the grandmother's version of a popular street food that can be found in many coastal villages.

4 cloves garlic, chopped
2.5cm (1in) piece galangal, chopped
4 candlenuts, chopped (see glossary)
4 red chillies, chopped
2 tsp ground coriander
salt and freshly ground black pepper
vegetable oil
500g (1lb) uncooked tiger prawns
1 stalk lemon grass, sliced
4 spring onions (scallions), chopped
2 tbsp tamarind water (see glossary)
4 tomatoes, chopped
2 kaffir lime leaves
$^1/_2$ cup coconut milk

place the garlic, galangal, candlenuts, chillies, coriander and a pinch of salt and pepper in a food processor or blender and blend to a paste.

heat a little vegetable oil in a heavy-based frying pan and fry the paste until fragrant, about 2–3 minutes. add the prawns and stir-fry until they have turned pink, about 3–4 minutes. add the remaining ingredients and simmer for 5 minutes.

serve with plain white rice.

3 cups coconut milk
$1/2$ cup tamarind water
(see glossary)
2.5cm (1in) piece
galangal, sliced
1 tsp ground coriander
1 tsp ground cumin
1 tsp ground turmeric
2 kaffir lime leaves
salt and freshly ground
black pepper
1.5 kg (3 lb) chicken, cut
into quarters
vegetable oil

Serves 4

500g (1lb) watercress
vegetable oil
1 tsp shrimp paste
(see glossary)
2 cloves garlic, chopped
2 spring onions
(scallions), sliced
1 red chilli, chopped
2 tbsp tamarind water
(see glossary)
2 tbsp kecap manis
(see glossary)
400ml (13fl.oz) coconut
cream
salt and freshly ground
black pepper

AYAM GORENG JOGYA
[yogyakarta-style fried chicken]

This is an excellent way to cook chicken. The poaching ensures succulent and flavoursome results, while the final grilling or frying encases the chicken in a crisp skin. On a return trip from the temples of Prambanam, I gorged myself at one of the many stalls excelling at this method.

combine the coconut milk, tamarind water, galangal, spices, lime leaves and a little salt and pepper in a large, heavy-based saucepan. add the chicken pieces and simmer until most of the liquid has been absorbed and the chicken is cooked through, about 1 hour.

allow the chicken to cool. brush with a little oil and barbecue on a very hot grill for a few minutes each side or, alternatively, deep-fry in oil until golden.

KANKUNG ASAM
[watercress in a sweet and sour sauce]

Waiting for the Trans-Sumatran bus of doom to arrive, I consumed a bowl of this most unusual dish while chatting to an old and wily corn peddler. Vendors naturally gravitate to where they will pick up the most business, and the very best of street food is often to be found at bus terminals and train stations.

wash and dry the watercress and set aside.

heat a little vegetable oil in a frying pan and fry the shrimp paste, garlic, spring onions and chilli for 2 minutes. add the watercress and stir-fry for 1 minute, then add the tamarind water, *kecap manis* and coconut cream. simmer for a few minutes and season to taste with salt and pepper. serve immediately.

[**note:** if watercress is unavailable, spinach may be used instead. omit the coconut cream if you prefer the dish less sweet.]

TAHU ISI
[tofu with savoury filling]

The Balinese love pork, and in the hills surrounding Ubud I was
fortunate enough to witness part of a traditional festival where
a whole pig was roasting over a spit barbecue. The celebrations
continued late into the night and well beyond my bedtime.
Yet the next day I saw the same man who had been tending the pig,
bright-eyed and bristling with energy, running a well-patronised stall
in town: **tahu isi** — *tofu stuffed with pork. Hmmm ...*

fry the garlic in a little oil, add the pork and cumin and continue stir-frying for 4–5 minutes. remove from heat and stir in the spring onions, coriander and the lightly beaten eggs.

gently scoop out the centre of each tofu block with a teaspoon and fill with the pork mixture. lightly dust with flour and fry carefully in 4–5cm (1^1/$_2$–2in) of oil, turning once, or steam for 20 minutes.

serve with **sambal kecap** (page 12).

Serves 6

2 cloves garlic, chopped
vegetable oil
200g (7oz) minced pork
1 tsp ground cumin
4 spring onions
(scallions), sliced
2 tbsp chopped coriander
leaves
2 eggs, lightly beaten
6 x 200g (7oz) blocks
fresh, firm tofu
plain flour, for dusting

PISANG GORENG
[banana fritters]

The most popular street food throughout Indonesia would have to be
these simple fritters. A sweet breakfast, an afternoon snack or a
late-night treat, they are available on almost every corner of the nation.
Should you happen to meet an Indonesian abroad, the mere mention
of **pisang goreng** *is sure to melt their heart and send their*
tongue into a patriotic frenzy.

combine the rice flour, salt, butter and coconut milk in a bowl and mix to a smooth batter. dip the bananas in the batter and deep-fry in very hot oil, in batches, until golden. drain on paper towels and, while still hot, roll in the caster sugar and cinnamon mixture. serve immediately.

Serves 6

150g (5oz) rice flour
pinch of salt
50g (2oz) butter, melted
1^1/$_2$ cups coconut milk
6 bananas, preferably
ladies' fingers or
cavendish, but not
plantains, sliced in half
lengthwise
vegetable oil or clarified
butter, for frying
^{1}/$_2$ cup caster sugar
mixed with 2 tsp
cinnamon

200g (7oz) glutinous
black rice (see glossary)
1 litre water
salt
6–7 cups coconut milk
4 tbsp brown sugar
2.5cm (1in) piece ginger,
sliced
4 cardamom pods, split
200g (7oz) green split
peas
2 sticks cinnamon
4 firm, ripe bananas,
sliced
$^1/_2$ cup shredded coconut,
toasted (see glossary)

BUBUR CAMPUR
[sticky black rice with coconut milk]

*In central Bali there is a magical place called Ubud. In the early
morning, as the steam rose from the surrounding rice paddies,
the creak of a hand-pushed cart signalled the approach of
bubur campur. I needed nothing more to prise me from bed,
running barefoot for my breakfast — as ambrosial and aromatic
a porridge as you will find anywhere in the world.*

rinse the rice under cold running water until the water runs clear. bring 1 litre water to the boil in a large pot, reduce to a simmer, and add the rice and a pinch of salt. cook until just done, about 30–40 minutes, checking every now and then to make sure it is not sticking to the bottom. when all the water has been absorbed, add enough coconut milk to cover the rice by 2.5cm (1in).

add 2 tablespoons of the sugar, plus the ginger and cardamom pods, and simmer for a further 30 minutes, adding more coconut milk if necessary. it should be the consistency of moist porridge.

meanwhile, rinse the split peas and place them in a pot of plenty of boiling, salted water. reduce heat and simmer very gently until just cooked, about 45 minutes. drain well.

in another pot, combine the remaining coconut milk and brown sugar, add the cinnamon sticks and cooked split peas and simmer gently for 15 minutes. add the sliced banana for the last 5 minutes. when ready, the mixture should be the consistency of a creamy sauce.

to serve, ladle a cup of the rice into a bowl, followed by a cup of the split pea and banana mix. top with toasted coconut.

malaysia

Malaysia is a rare combination.
Sharing the same language and many of the same
customs with its neighbour Indonesia,
Malaysian culture is a woven tapestry
of Chinese merchants, southern Indian immigrants
(predominantly from Tamil Nadu),
Thais and, of course, the indigenous Malays,
who themselves evolved from island-hopping
and Southeast Asian migration.

The multicultural meccas of Kuala Lumpur and Georgetown are true melting pots of diversity. Georgetown, although not indicative of the entire Malay population, is where I spent most of my time. Its streets are a confusion of frenzied, cross-cultural intentions and its street-food vendors are a delicious mirror of this mayhem.

The most prominent influence arrived with the legions of Chinese, who brought with them the traditional cooking styles of braised meats, steamed seafood and stir-fries – almost an antithesis to the cuisine of the Indians and their slow-cooked stews and flat-breads. Yet there is harmony amongst the cacophony in the way they share the streets. Whether it's the banana leaf 'rice and meals' of the Hindu south, the korma-style curries (rich with spices, nuts and dried fruits) from the Muslim north, the Cantonese steamed dumplings of fiery Sichuan noodles, the choice is bewildering.

Malaysia, owing to its history of successive immigration and colonisation, is a country with distinctive provincial characteristics. In the south there is the undeniable connection with the cuisine of Java, most notably in their use of peanuts and sweet soy sauce, while a common religion means they share the same dietary restrictions of their southern neighbours. Islam discourages the consumption of pork, while other meats must follow a strict method of preparation known as *halal*.

There are many culinary crossover points between the Malay and the Indonesians. Some dishes are claimed by both parties and since I am no expert on that matter, I simply cite a dish in whatever country I consumed or enjoyed it the most. **Saté** is one such dish: I lip-smacked my way around the lamb and chicken versions in Indonesia, drooled over a mixed seafood variation in Singapore and devoured a deliciously Middle Eastern-style ground beef one in Malaysia. **Rendang** is another example whose origins may be Malay, yet I have chosen to list it in the Indonesian section. Then again, **biriyani** is Indian and you'll find that under Singapore, and the Chinese staple **congee**, you'll discover in this chapter on Malaysia. The process from imitation through integration to innovation is what makes the culinary quagmire so fascinating.

The south is also home to Melaka, the capital of the district and, up until the end of the nineteenth century, the main port of commerce. Melaka still wears its Portuguese, Dutch and English influences in its architecture, but the over-riding culinary invasion occurred before all of these with the arrival in 1405 of Admiral Cheng Ho – the 'three jewelled eunuch prince' of the Chinese Ming Dynasty. Consequent intermarriages between immigrants and locals led to a hybrid cuisine – Nonya. Predominantly Chinese in style, it uses some of the spices more common to Indian cuisine, such as turmeric, cumin, coriander, cloves, cinnamon and cardamom, while the generous addition of coconut, chilli, fragrant roots and aromatic leaves make up the indigenous contribution. Although thought of as more akin to home cooking, Nonya cuisine is attracting an increasing amount of international recognition for **laksa lemak**, a spicy coconut noodle dish and other specialities such as **otak otak**, fish cakes grilled in pandanus or banana leaves.

The north tends towards a Thai influence with the sourness of tamarind and lime. Coconut is prevalent throughout Malaysia: in the north it is added to

soup-like curries to balance the sour-ness, while in the south they add coconut to create thick, rich gravies.

Malaysia is also home to an abun-dance of tropical fruit, the most controversial of which is the *durian* – a large fruit, like an oval or tear-shaped medicine ball, with a hard green and ferociously spiny exterior. To crack one open is to assault your olfactory nerves with a most hideous odour. The taste, if one can separate the two senses, is actually quite delicious, but consid-ering the profusion of mangoes, pawpaw (papaya), bananas and pineapples, many people forego the reek and satisfy themselves with the familiar. Other exotic fruits of note are the *rambutan* – a small red pouch covered with soft furry spikes, revealing an opaque fruit very much like the lychee; the *mangosteen* – a segmented white-fleshed fruit with a brown and purple skin; and one of my favourites, the *jackfruit* or *nangka* – a large, spiky green fruit which has hundreds of black seeds housed inside delicious, fleshy, yellow segments. Small plastic bags of these are sold at train and bus stations, and a common dessert features these cooked in coconut milk and palm sugar.

The *pasar malam* (night market) in Georgetown boasts an array of hawkers from the entire spectrum of the Malaysian population. The aromas hypnotise, and I would find myself returning night after night to my favourite stalls. Although there is some similar activity during the day, I rather fancy that it's balmy evenings that make the night markets such a feature. Of course, the function doesn't stop at just providing nourishment; one can also find electrical goods, the latest in Malay pop, clothes, fabrics, toiletries

and hardware. Yet it's the food and the social interaction that most Malays come for. In a country where there are few bars (Islam forbids the consumption of alcohol) and even fewer nightclubs, the night markets are where young people come to fraternise and families to socialise. And all this occurs while the Chinese hawkers throw around a variety of noodles, the Indians toss the dough for their **roti chanais** and the indigenous Malays fan the coals under their banana-leaf parcels.

A typical stall could consist of an entire family at work: an old man whose shaky hands can still form the perfect curry puff; a young mother with a baby slung over her back, gently frying little cres-cent-moon pastries, while her eldest son works up a sweat in the humidity as he kneads the dough for the next batch. Somewhere in the background the fruit blenders whirr continuously, whipping up icy tropical cocktails, while the bells of the bicycle rickshaws have a distant, almost mystical call like love-sick wind chimes. Malaysia's *pasar malam*'s are a place full of noisy good cheer, bright lights and tantalising smells – a great venue to be an enthralled spectator, for they are a true theatre of life.

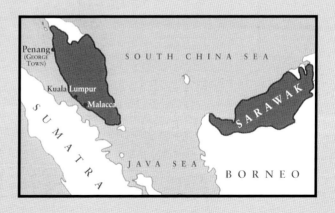

21

2.5cm (1in) piece
galangal, sliced
1 onion, chopped
2 red chillies, chopped
1 stalk lemon grass,
sliced
4 candlenuts
2 kaffir lime leaves
$1/4$ cup coconut milk
500g (1lb) perch or ling
fillets
2 tbsp cornflour
2 eggs
2 tbsp chopped
coriander leaves
1 tsp ground cumin
1 tsp ground turmeric
salt and freshly ground
black pepper
banana leaves or
pandanus leaves
(see glossary)
or aluminium foil

OTAK OTAK
[fish cakes grilled in banana leaves]

*Banana leaves and pandanus leaves impart a wonderful aroma to rice,
and when grilled over a fire they lend a slightly smoky flavour to
the food. Malaysian street vendors seem never to cook over an
open flame: they wait until the coals are glowing and,
when a customer gives the nod to go ahead, they gently fan
the embers to produce just the right amount of heat.*

place the galangal, onion, chillies, lemon grass, candlenuts and lime leaves in a food processor or blender and blend to a thick paste, adding just enough coconut milk to thin out any lumps. add the remaining ingredients, except the banana leaves, and pulse until everything is well incorporated, but still slightly chunky.

cut the banana leaves into twelve 25cm (10in) squares and blanch for 2 minutes.

place a generous tablespoon of mixture in the centre of each square and fold into a parcel. secure with a toothpick, brush with oil and grill on the barbecue for 10–15 minutes on each side or until the fishcakes are firm and slightly browned.

serve when the parcels are cool enough to handle.

[**note**: if banana leaves are not available, you can cook the fish cakes in a frying pan with a little oil until lightly golden and slightly crisp on the outside.]

OPPOSITE: **otak otak** — fish cakes grilled in banana leaves

LUMPIA
[spring rolls]

The Malaysians may not have invented them —
they're definitely courtesy of Chinese immigrants —
but these spring rolls are the tastiest I've ever eaten.

2 tsp vegetable oil
3 cloves garlic, chopped
2.5cm (1in) piece ginger, chopped
250g (8oz) uncooked prawns, chopped
100g ($3^1/_2$oz) minced pork
100g ($3^1/_2$oz) carrots, cut into thin strips
2 tbsp soy sauce
salt and freshly ground black pepper
100g ($3^1/_2$oz) bean sprouts
100g ($3^1/_2$oz) cellophane noodles, soaked in water for 10 minutes and cut into 2cm ($^3/_4$in) lengths
2 tbsp chopped coriander leaves
4 spring onions (scallions), chopped
1 egg, beaten
1 packet large spring roll wrappers (about 20)
1 extra beaten egg
vegetable oil, for deep-frying

heat the vegetable oil in a frying pan and fry the garlic and ginger for 2 minutes. add the prawns, pork, carrots and soy sauce and cook for a further 3 minutes. season to taste with salt and pepper and remove from heat. transfer to a bowl and, when cool, mix in the bean sprouts, noodles, coriander, spring onions and egg.

lay out the spring roll wrappers on a flat surface and place 2 tablespoons of the mixture in the bottom left-hand corner of each wrapper. pull the corner over the filling and roll up the wrapper, folding the two side flaps towards the middle. brush the top corner with a little beaten egg to seal. deep-fry the rolls in very hot oil until golden. drain on paper towels.

serve immediately.

OPPOSITE: **rendang daging** — rich beef curry [page 10]

TAHU GORENG
[fried tofu with bean sprouts and sweet tamarind sauce]

TAMARIND SAUCE
1 tbsp sesame oil
1 tsp shrimp paste
2 cloves garlic, crushed
5cm (2in) piece ginger, grated
1 cup tamarind water (see glossary)
2 tbsp kecap manis *(see glossary)*
1 tbsp brown sugar

FRIED TOFU
vegetable oil, for deep-frying
500g (1lb) block of firm tofu, cut into 6 squares
1 cup plain flour

GARNISH
1 punnet bean sprouts
coriander leaves
6 birdseye chillies, split down the middle
2 tbsp roasted peanuts, chopped

to make the tamarind sauce, heat the sesame oil in a wok and fry the shrimp paste until fragrant, about 1 minute. add the garlic and ginger and stir-fry for a further minute, then add the tamarind water, *kecap manis* and sugar. bring to the boil, reduce heat to a simmer and cook until the sauce is slightly thickened, about 15 minutes. remove from heat.

meanwhile, in a heavy-based saucepan, heat the oil until just smoking. roll the tofu in flour, dust off any excess and gently lower into the oil. turn if necessary and fry until golden. drain on paper towels.

pour a ladleful of tamarind sauce into six small bowls. place a piece of the tofu in the centre, top with bean sprouts, a few coriander leaves and a birdseye chilli. sprinkle with chopped peanuts and serve.

SATÉ DAGING LEMBU
[beef satay]

Rectangular boxes of hot coals surrounded him. Amidst the smoke
the hands worked, turning one skewer, dabbing a little marinade on
another, while still other hands seemed to appear simultaneously
offering sticks of glistening satay to yet another drooling customer.
I couldn't help thinking of those garish posters depicting the
Indian god Siva in the dance of perpetual motion,
tridents and conch shells flailing in each of his eight hands.

combine all the ingredients for the meat patties in a large bowl and mix with your hands until everything is well incorporated. mould the mixture around each skewer, making sausage shapes about 2cm ($^3/_4$in) thick. brush with a little oil. cook on the barbecue, in a char-grill pan or under an overhead grill, turning the skewers a little at a time until all sides are well cooked, about 4–5 minutes.

brush with the marinade, return to the grill for 20 seconds each side and serve immediately.

MARINADE: bring the soy sauce and sugar to the boil. reduce heat to a simmer, add the tamarind extract and continue cooking until mixture thickens. remove from heat, stir in the sesame oil and set aside.

[
note: if you prefer the peanut sauce that accompanies most satay, you will find the recipe on page 7.
]

500g (1lb) minced beef
1 onion, diced
2 cloves garlic, crushed
5cm (2in) piece ginger, grated
1 tsp shrimp paste, grilled (see glossary)
1 spring onion (scallion), finely sliced
1 tsp ground cumin
1 tsp ground turmeric
1 tsp ground cardamom
1 tsp ground cloves
1 tsp chilli powder
$^1/_2$ cup roasted peanuts, chopped
$^1/_2$ bunch coriander roots, finely chopped
1 egg, beaten
1 tbsp plain flour
salt and freshly ground black pepper

16 wooden skewers, soaked in water for a few hours

MARINADE
$^1/_4$ cup soy sauce
4 tbsp brown sugar
1 cup tamarind water (see glossary)
2 tbsp sesame oil

27

2 cups long-grain
white rice
4–5 pandanus leaves
(see glossary)
4 cups coconut cream
5cm (2in) piece ginger,
sliced
1 spring onion
(scallion), sliced
salt, to taste
water

GARNISH
2 hard-boiled eggs, sliced
1 cucumber, sliced
4 tsp **sambal ikan bilis**
2 spring onions
(scallions), sliced
handful of roasted
peanuts
4 sprigs coriander

NASI LEMAK
[coconut rice with condiments]

Nasi lemak *is a delicious staple, included in the repertoire of most Malaysian street vendors. Although the numerous variations make this a dish of multiple personalities, it is almost universally served with* **sambal ikan bilis** *(see recipe opposite) and garnished with boiled eggs, peanuts and cucumbers. Ahhh ... but there is lemak and there's* **lemak,** *and customer loyalty speaks volumes for quality — there was one very stern woman whose morning trade (yes, it's a breakfast favourite) convinced me to join the queue.*

wash the rice thoroughly under cold running water, then soak for 15 minutes in water to cover. drain well. put the rice, pandanus leaves, coconut cream, ginger, spring onion and a little salt in a heavy-based saucepan and bring to the boil. reduce heat to a very gentle simmer, cover with a tight-fitting lid, and cook until the rice is done, about 12–15 minutes, adding a little water if necessary.

to serve, press the rice into a small bowl, then unmould it in the centre of each serving plate. surround with hard-boiled egg, cucumber, a heaped tablespoon of **sambal ikan bilis,** and top with spring onions, peanuts and a sprig of coriander.

SAMBAL IKAN BILIS
[chilli fish]

Makes about 1½ cups

heat half the oil in a wok and fry the *ikan bilis* until crisp. drain and set aside.

grind the shrimp paste, garlic, spring onion and chillies using a mortar and pestle, or blend using a food processor, until they form a smooth paste.

heat the remaining 1 tablespoon of oil in a wok and fry the paste until fragrant, about 3–4 minutes. add the onion rings and fry until translucent, then add the sugar, salt and tamarind water and continue to cook until the sauce thickens. remove from heat, stir in the *ikan bilis* and serve with **nasi lemak** (see recipe opposite). keeps in the refrigerator for up to two weeks.

2 tbsp vegetable oil
1 cup ikan bilis *(see glossary)* or dried anchovies
1 tbsp shrimp paste *(see glossary)*
3 cloves garlic, chopped
1 spring onion (scallion), sliced
10 small dried red chillies, soaked in 1 cup warm water for 10 minutes and drained
2 large onions, sliced into rings
1 tbsp brown sugar
1 tsp salt
4 tbsp tamarind water *(see glossary)*

Serves 6

250g (8oz) uncooked
tiger prawns
1 fresh medium blue
swimmer crab
250g (8oz) mussels or
clams (pippies)
1 large squid hood
2 medium gemfish
fillets or other firm,
white-fleshed fish
500g (1lb) rice vermicelli
1 tbsp vegetable oil
4 cups water
5cm (20in) piece
galangal, thickly sliced
4 kaffir lime leaves
1 stalk lemon grass, cut
diagonally into 1cm
($^1/_3$in) lengths
4 cups coconut milk
$^1/_2$ cup vietnamese mint
or coriander leaves

PASTE
2 cloves garlic
4 spring onions
(scallions), white part
only, sliced
2 tsp sesame oil
1 tsp shrimp paste,
grilled
(see glossary)
4 red chillies, chopped
4 candlenuts
1 bunch coriander roots
1 tsp ground turmeric
1 tsp ground cumin
1 tsp salt
1 tsp brown sugar

LAKSA LEMAK
[coconut noodle soup with seafood]

There are two main varieties of **laksa:** *the hot and sour* **assam,** *with its fragrant bite of tamarind, that originates in Georgetown, and this wickedly rich version, perhaps the best-known example of Nonya cuisine. I have purposely made this the 'deluxe' version, which is one of the bonuses of street food — you simply point to whatever ingredients you want included. It can be served as a starter or a main, to be slurped and spilt, brimming with whatever seafood you can get your hands on. And it's just as tasty if only fish or prawns are used!*

shell and devein the prawns; reserve the heads. clean the crab by removing the two front claws, splitting the body into quarters and removing the intestines. scrub the mussels and remove the beards. soak the mussels in a bowl of water for 10 minutes, then steam them open in a saucepan with $^1/_2$ cup boiling water, shaking vigorously every few minutes. discard any that do not open. wash the squid hood, score the flesh in a criss-cross pattern and slice into 4 x 2cm ($^3/_4$in) strips. cut the fish into 3cm ($1^1/_4$in) cubes.

soak the rice vermicelli in cold water for 20 minutes, then drain.

place the paste ingredients in a food processor or blender and blend until smooth.

heat the vegetable oil in a wok or frying pan and fry the prawn heads until bright pink. discard the heads, add the paste and continue to fry for 2–3 minutes, add the water, galangal, kaffir lime leaves and lemon grass and simmer for 15 minutes. add the coconut milk and simmer for a further 5 minutes. gently place the crab in the soup and cook for 5 minutes. add the fish cubes and cook for a further 5 minutes, then add the prawns, squid and mussels. continue to cook until the prawns turn pink. remove from heat.

place half a cup of rice vermicelli in each serving bowl and ladle the soup over the top. using tongs, divide the seafood equally among the bowls, sprinkle with vietnamese mint or coriander and serve.

LAKSA ASSAM

[spicy sour noodle soup with fish]

Serves 6

cut the fish into 2cm (³/₄in) cubes. soak the noodles in boiling water for 5 minutes, then drain.

heat the sesame oil in a large wok over high heat and fry the shrimp paste until fragrant, about 1 minute, stirring constantly. add the turmeric, cumin and garlic and fry for 1 minute.

pour in the water and bring to the boil, then reduce heat to a gentle simmer. add the fish sauce, tamarind water, galangal, kaffir lime leaves, lemon grass and chillies and simmer for 15 minutes. add the fish pieces and continue to simmer until just cooked, about 8–10 minutes. check seasoning and remove from heat.

divide the noodles equally among 6 serving bowls and ladle soup over the top. garnish with spring onions and coriander leaves.

*2 medium gemfish fillets
or other firm,
white-fleshed fish
500g (1lb) wide, flat rice
noodles
1 tbsp sesame oil
1 tsp shrimp paste
1 tsp ground turmeric
1 tsp ground cumin
2 cloves garlic, chopped
4 cups water
¹/₄ cup fish sauce
(see glossary)
¹/₂ cup tamarind water
(see glossary)
5cm (2in) piece galangal,
thickly sliced
4 kaffir lime leaves
1 stalk lemon grass, cut
diagonally into 1cm
(¹/₃in) lengths
2 red chillies, chopped
salt and freshly ground
black pepper
2 spring onions
(scallions), sliced
diagonally into 2cm
(³/₄in) lengths
2 tbsp chopped coriander
leaves*

31

*250g (8oz) short-grain
rice*
*2.5 litres (4pts) chicken
stock or water*
1/4 cup dried shrimp
1 tbsp soy sauce
1 tbsp rice wine vinegar
salt and white pepper
*1 tbsp finely sliced
spring onion*
*1 tbsp finely chopped
coriander*

GARNISH
*a selection of pickles
(bamboo shoots, bean
sprouts)*
slices of hard-boiled eggs
any leftovers whatsoever!

CONGEE
[savoury rice soup]

Congee *or zhou, (pronounced 'jow'), is a Chinese dish consisting of
little more than rice cooked in flavoured stock to a point where the
grains fall apart and the consistency is similar to that of porridge.
It is very soothing and easy to digest, and is often fed to the
old and sick. However, it is one of the most popular street-side snacks at
breakfast, when the body has not fully woken up, and at supper,
when a little warmth in the belly is preferred to a rousing main meal.
Wherever there's a strong contingent of ethnic Chinese
(as in the bustling markets of Georgetown), one will find* **congee.**

place the rice and stock in a heavy-based saucepan, bring to the boil, then reduce heat to a very gentle simmer. stir occasionally to check the rice is not sticking to the bottom of the pan. when the rice has been cooking for about $1^1/_2$ hours, add the dried prawns, soy sauce and rice wine vinegar and continue to cook for a further 30 minutes. season to taste with salt and pepper.

serve in small bowls with a sprinkle of shallots and coriander on top. offer a selection of condiments for each person to add as they like.

HINOMPULA
[tapioca coconut pudding]

Serves 6

A tiny, high-pitched bell announced her arrival, both first thing in the morning and at the end of every day. Winding her way around the narrow streets, she pushed a flat-top cart that was divided into two sections, offering a choice of two mouthwatering sweets: black rice pudding, similar to the Indonesian **bubur campur** *on page 18, and* **hinompula***. Somewhat lighter than the rice pudding, the tapioca* **hinompula** *was my favourite, and if I wasn't quick enough to catch her the first time around, it was always the first to disappear.*

200g (7oz) packet tapioca
400ml (13fl.oz) can coconut cream
1 pandanus leaf (see glossary)
pinch of salt
1 stick cinnamon
4 cardamom pods, split
$1/2$ cup palm sugar
juice and grated rind of 2 limes
100g ($3^1/2$oz) shredded coconut, lightly toasted (see glossary)
100g ($3^1/2$oz) roasted peanuts, coarsely chopped

wash and drain the tapioca and place it in a heavy-based saucepan with the coconut cream, pandanus leaf and salt. bring to the boil, then reduce heat to a very gentle simmer. add the cinnamon stick, cardamom pods and palm sugar and cook, stirring, until the tapioca has swollen and turned opaque. (if necessary add water to the pot to stop the tapioca sticking). stir in the lime juice and rind. remove from heat.

pour the tapioca into a 20cm x 20cm (8in x 8in) baking tray, remove the cinnamon stick and cardamom pods and spread the mixture evenly to a thickness of 4–5cm ($1^1/2$–2in).

sprinkle with the coconut and peanuts, cover with plastic wrap and refrigerate until set. cut into squares and serve.

singapore

Few countries offer a more varied culinary experience than Singapore. While the population is predominantly Chinese (78 per cent), the influence of the Malay and Indian communities is everywhere and the diversity continues, albeit to a lesser extent, with the Vietnamese, Thai, Japanese and Korean immigrants.

To top it all off, Singapore's geographical position as the gateway to Southeast Asia means there is a constant flow of western business and pleasure-seekers to cater for, as well as the relics of the British empire and the regal demands of a prominent ex-pat community. Yet the street food in Singapore is so much more than the sum of all its parts. What makes the hawkers of Singapore so dynamic is that they are continually evolving their craft, blending their influences and trading their methods, produce and spices back and forth – true merchants within the culture of street food.

For Singaporeans, food is a national pastime. In fact it has become one of Singapore's main tourist attractions and as such, an industry in itself. Chefs from all over the world are drawn to the island nation for ever bigger pay cheques and the country's insatiable desire to impress. This only adds to Singapore's reputation as a place on the cutting edge of food as culture.

The hawker centres in Singapore are unsurpassed for their flurried activity and assortment of culinary styles. In a city where space is at a premium, many of these markets have been moved off the narrow sidewalks and into car parks – proving necessity is truly the father of invention. As opposed to the more anarchic markets of their neighbours, Singapore's street food is somewhat systematic and a little more obedient to the government's obsession with law and order. Stalls are semi-permanent and crammed in lines, a bit like a culinary sideshow alley where hawkers from a dozen different backgrounds vie for your patronage.

To see the Indians ply their trade amongst the Chinese, Malay and Vietnamese stall holders, it's difficult not to notice the competition at work. Each has their own loyal patronage, usually from the same home turf as the cook, and yet they are quite capable of living side by side, stealing, borrowing and begging the secrets of each other's cuisine and blending them into Southeast Asia's most diverse kitchen.

In between the rows of hawkers is a confusion of mismatched tables and stools. It doesn't matter where you sit or from what stall you order – share a table and you will be surrounded by authentic dishes from half a dozen countries. The aromas are intoxicating, and the colour and noise add to the ambience of a truly Singaporean experience.

Food is not the only benefit these centres provide. They are in fact a great unifying forum, providing common ground for the entire spectrum of Singapore's population: in a single sitting one could easily encounter high-tech executives barking into mobile phones, women in traditional Muslim scarves whispering in hushed tones, rowdy children tucking into steaming bowls of **congee** and a majestically turbaned Sikh combing the **paratha** pastry from his moustache. From the offal of endangered species to the abundant Singapore noodles, the hawker centres of Singapore offer a unique combination of restaurant-quality food in next to no time, and all for the price of a glass of beer. (And on that subject, Singapore lager is one of the finest drops in Southeast Asia).

Along with these myriad cultures comes the festivals. In Singapore there is nothing that surpasses Chinese New Year for pageantry, celebration and feasting. The Chinese community also celebrate the Qing Ming Festival (in honour of ancestors) and the Mooncake Festival (sweet and savoury-filled cakes signify the full moon and a cycle completed).

The Indian community's (mainly Hindus and Sikhs) major celebration is Deepavali – the Festival of Lights. The Muslims and Malays celebrate Hari Raya Puasa at the end of Ramadan, and Hari Raya Haji to celebrate the convergence of Haj pilgrims to Mecca. The Buddhists celebrate Vesak Day in honour of the enlightenment of Buddha. Then, of course there is the commercially driven Christmas and Easter celebrations where most of the festivity seems to take place over cash registers at the larger department stores. Because all these faiths are so strongly followed, the demand for traditional produce is well catered for – Singapore's grocery stores and vegetable markets are a remarkable study in racial integration.

Squeezed between the sky-hungry high-rises, the hawker centres of Singapore are a kaleidoscope of action and a fusion of styles, a vivid and vital cultural affair that parades the very best of what street food has to offer.

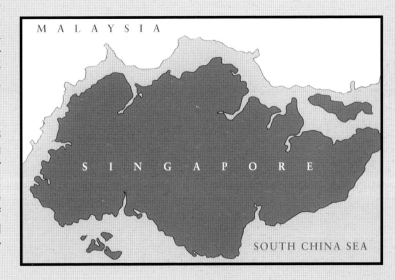

MALAYSIA

SINGAPORE

SOUTH CHINA SEA

SESAME PRAWN SKEWERS

20 large uncooked tiger
prawns or uncooked
king prawns
20 wooden skewers,
soaked in water for
1 hour
1 lime, cut into wedges
(optional)

MARINADE
1 tbsp vegetable oil
1 tbsp sesame oil
2 tbsp soy sauce
1 tbsp palm sugar
or brown sugar
2 cloves garlic, crushed
5cm (2in) piece ginger,
grated
2 small red chillies,
finely chopped
2 tsp salt
2 tsp freshly ground
black pepper
2 tbsp sesame seeds
1/2 bunch coriander
leaves, finely chopped
juice of 1 lime

There's nothing quite so stunning as a giant prawn threaded onto a
skewer, glistening and crispy, straight from the char-grill
— the consummate culinary fashion statement!

remove the legs from the prawns but keep the shells, heads and tails intact. (this helps seal in the flavour when the prawns are barbecued, and the crispy shell adds to the texture). devein the prawns by making a small incision in the back and using a toothpick or skewer to dig under the vein and lift it out. make a slit down the stomach — this helps stop the prawn from curling on the skewer.

combine the marinade ingredients in a bowl, making sure that the sugar is well dissolved. marinate the prawns in this mixture for 1 hour.

thread each prawn, tail first, lengthwise onto a skewer, keeping the prawn as straight as possible, and stopping just below the head. char-grill for 2–3 minutes each side, turning once, or until the prawns turn a deep pink and the shells become crisp and a little blackened. serve immediately: if desired, ease the prawn a little further down the skewer and top with a wedge of lime.

ROTI CHANAI
[stuffed indian-style bread]

*There are myriad variations on this simple dish: the filling can be
a curried potato or cauliflower mixture, for example,
and the method of cooking can alter the taste. Known as* dhalpuri
when deep-fried or stuffed, and paratha *when the bread is designed
to be more like a flaky pastry,* **roti** *is as versatile and imaginative
as the mind that creates it.*

Serves 6

FILLING
*450g (15oz) yellow split
peas, washed and
drained
1 tsp salt
1 tsp ground turmeric
1 tbsp ghee
1 onion, diced
1 tbsp brown mustard
seeds
1 tbsp cumin seeds*

ROTI
*750g (1^1/$_2$lb) plain flour
6 tsp baking powder
1 tsp salt
100g (3^1/$_2$oz) ghee,
softened
2 cups water
(approximately)*

place the split peas in a saucepan with plenty of water and add the salt and turmeric. bring to the boil then reduce to a simmer. skim any scum from the surface and cook until the peas are soft, about 30 minutes. drain and allow to cool.

heat the ghee in a frying pan and gently fry the onion, mustard seeds and cumin seeds until the onion is translucent. combine this mixture with the split peas and refrigerate until ready to use — preferably up to 6 hours.

sift the flour, baking powder and salt into a large mixing bowl and rub in the ghee until the mixture looks like small breadcrumbs. add the water a little at a time, mixing with your fingers, until a soft dough forms. transfer the dough to a floured surface and knead for 7–8 minutes. form into balls 5cm (2in) in diameter and roll out on a floured surface into rounds approximately 1cm (^{1}/$_3$in) thick.

place 2 tablespoons of the split pea and onion filling in the centre of the rounds and, gathering from all sides, close the dough over the top, sealing well. roll out gently on a floured surface to a diameter of 10–12cm (4–5in). brush one side of the **roti** with extra ghee and place this side down in a large, heavy-based frying pan. cook until lightly browned, about 3–4 minutes, then brush the other side with ghee, turn over and repeat. wrap in a warm tea towel until you have cooked all the **rotis**.

37

MIXED SEAFOOD SATAY

*500g (1lb) white fish
fillets (snapper,
perch or ling)*
*200g (7oz) uncooked
prawns, shelled and
deveined*
2 tbsp cornflour
1 egg, beaten
*salt and freshly ground
black pepper*
10–15 stalks lemon grass
1 lime, cut into wedges

PASTE
2 cloves garlic, chopped
*5cm (2in) piece ginger,
chopped*
4 candlenuts
1 tsp ground cumin
1 tsp ground turmeric
1 tsp ground coriander
1 red chilli, chopped
2 tbsp brown sugar
*2 tbsp chopped coriander
leaves*

*In this recipe, lemon grass is used in place of skewers.
They impart a magnificent fragrance to the satay and give a
tangy lift to the flavour. Choose strong, fresh stalks that will
handle the heat of a grill without wilting.*

place the paste ingredients in a food processor or blender and blend well. add the fish fillets and prawns, and pulse until the paste has a slightly lumpy consistency but is well combined. transfer the paste to a large bowl, add the cornflour and beaten egg, season to taste with salt and pepper and mix well.

remove any of the green section from the lemon grass that may wilt under heat. cut the rest in half crosswise — there should be at least 15cm (6in) per half. if the root end is quite thick, slice it lengthwise to produce another skewer.

take a handful of the seafood mixture and mould it around the lemon grass to form a sausage. brush with a little oil and grill on a barbecue or in a char-grill pan until golden — the sugar will caramelise slightly, adding to the flavour. serve immediately with a squeeze of lime and, if desired, some white rice and **bumbu saté** (page 7).

CHICKEN BIRIYANI
[indian-style rice pilaf]

Serves 4

A dish with roots in southern Indian cuisine ...
prepared by a Malaysian woman with a distinctive Nonya touch ...
served in the neon chaos of a hawker centre
— couldn't be anywhere but Singapore.

grind the garlic, salt, ginger, chillies and nuts using a mortar and pestle, or blend in a food processor or blender.

in a wok or a frying pan with a lid, heat the ghee and gently fry the spices, onion, red pepper and spring onion. add the meat and fry until brown. stir in the ground or blended ingredients and continue to stir until fragrant, adding a little water if necessary. cover tightly and cook for 10–12 minutes.

put the rice and coconut milk in a large, heavy-based pan with a tight-fitting lid and add water to cover by 2.5cm (1in). bring to the boil, then reduce heat to the lowest setting, cover tightly and steam. once the rice has absorbed all the liquid (this should take about 10 minutes), make a large well in the centre of the rice and spoon in the meat mixture. cover tightly and cook over very low heat until the rice is cooked, about 10–15 minutes.

serve straight from the pan, or stir very gently, pile onto plates and top with a piece of meat.

2 cloves garlic, chopped
1 tsp salt
5cm (2in) piece ginger, chopped
2 small red chillies, chopped
1 cup mixed almonds and cashews
4 tbsp ghee
4 cloves
1 tsp cumin seeds
1 tsp ground coriander
2 tsp ground turmeric
1 stick cinnamon
1 onion, diced
1 red pepper, diced
1 spring onion (scallion), sliced
1.5kg (3lb) chicken, cut into 8 pieces or 750g (1^1/$_2$lb) beef or lamb, cubed
450g (15oz) basmati or long-grain rice, washed well and drained
400ml (14fl.oz) can coconut milk
water

CHILLI CRAB

4 fresh blue
swimmer crabs
1 cup tamarind water,
preferably made with the
water in which the crabs
are boiled (see glossary)
2 tbsp vegetable oil
1 tbsp brown
mustard seeds
3 onions, chopped
4 cloves garlic,
very finely chopped
5cm (2in) piece ginger,
grated
4 birdseye chillies,
finely sliced
1 tsp ground turmeric
1 tsp ground coriander
2 tbsp sugar
1 tsp cornflour mixed
with 1/2 cup water
1/2 bunch spring onions
(scallions), sliced
diagonally

*Variations on this classic are only limited
by the imagination, so go wild.*

bring a large pot of water to the boil and drop in the crabs. cook for no longer than 4 minutes. remove the crabs, reserving 1 cup of liquid to soak the tamarind. chop the crabs into quarters and crack the claws and larger legs.

heat the vegetable oil in a large wok. add the mustard seeds and stir until they pop, then add the onions, garlic, ginger, chillies, turmeric and coriander. when fragrant, add the crab pieces and stir to coat. strain the tamarind water into the wok and simmer for 4–5 minutes.

transfer the crab pieces to a serving platter. add the sugar and the cornflour mixture to the wok and stir until the sauce thickens. pour the sauce over the crab pieces and garnish with spring onions.

OPPOSITE: **sesame prawn skewers** (page 36)

FISH-HEAD CURRY

A marriage of Indian and Nonya cuisine, fish-head curry probably
originated as a result of meagre earnings — while the fillets from the
largest catch went to those who could afford them, the less affluent
would race down to the markets to grab the prized leftover: the head of
the fish. To those who might shudder at this, I can only say one thing — try it!
Without doubt, the most delicious flesh of a large fish is the
area immediately behind the head and, believe it or not, the cheek.
Eaten with plenty of plain white rice, this is a complete meal and is
considered one of Singapore's specialties. Traditionally this dish is
cooked over low flames in a clay pot that is then carried to the table.

to make the paste, grind all the paste ingredients in a mortar, or blend in a food processor or blender until smooth.

carefully open the cans of coconut milk and skim off the thick 'cream' at the top — about 4 tablespoons. reserve remaining milk. heat the cream in a wide, deep, heavy-based saucepan, add the paste and cook, stirring, until fragrant, about 3–4 minutes, taking care not to let the mixture burn. add the onions and cook, stirring, for 2 minutes. reduce heat to low, place the fish heads in the bottom of the pan and pour over enough water to cover by 5cm (2in). add the galangal, tamarind water, curry leaves, tomatoes and cardamom, put the lid on the pot and simmer for 15 minutes.

pour in the remaining coconut milk, and if more liquid is required, pour in just enough water to cover the fish. add half the spring onions and the coriander roots, replace the lid and cook for a further 10 minutes. when the heads are almost falling apart, remove from heat and gently transfer to a heated clay pot or serving bowl. sprinkle with the remaining spring onions and the coriander leaves and serve with plenty of plain white rice.

OPPOSITE: **gai yang nam jim gai wan** — char-grilled sweet chilli chicken (page 57)

2 x 400ml (14fl.oz) cans
coconut milk (do not
shake before opening)
2 large onions, thickly
sliced
2–3 large fish heads,
preferably snapper or red
emperor
4 cups water
5cm (2in) piece galangal,
sliced
1 cup tamarind water
(see glossary)
4 curry leaves
2 medium tomatoes,
chopped
4 cardamom pods, split
2 spring onions
(scallions), sliced
1/2 bunch coriander,
roots finely chopped,
leaves reserved for
garnish

PASTE
4 candlenuts
2 cloves garlic, chopped
4 spring onions
(scallions), white part
only, sliced
2 tsp sesame oil
1 tsp shrimp paste
(see glossary)
4 red chillies, seeded and
chopped
2 tsp ground turmeric
1 tsp ground cumin
1 tsp garam masala
1 tsp salt

MURTABAK
[stuffed indian-style crepes]

Watching a street vendor spinning **murtabak** *dough and throwing it*
against a stainless steel kneading surface is not unlike witnessing a
pizza proprietor from Naples. However, its soft texture and
enclosed filling mean **murtabak** *is closer to the French crepe than a*
pizza. The classic **murtabak** *is very thin — almost translucent*
— and is suited to any savoury or sweet filling you care to try.

DOUGH

1 ¹/₂ *cups* atta *(see glossary) or plain flour*
¹/₂ *tsp salt*
¹/₂ *tsp garam masala*
¹/₂ *cup warm water*
2 *tsp vegetable oil, plus extra*
1 *egg, lightly beaten*

FILLING

1 *tbsp vegetable oil*
1 *small onion, diced*
1 *clove garlic, finely chopped*
2.5cm *(1in) piece ginger, grated*
¹/₂ *tsp ground turmeric*
¹/₂ *tsp chilli powder*
250g *(8oz) minced lamb*
salt

DOUGH: sift the flour, salt and garam masala into a large bowl. mix the water and 2 teaspoons of oil together and add to the flour. knead the dough for at least 15 minutes to develop its elasticity, then divide into 6 balls of equal size, roll in oil, cover with a damp tea towel and allow to stand for 1 hour.

FILLING: heat the oil in a frying pan and fry the onion, garlic and ginger until the onion is translucent. add the turmeric and chilli and cook, stirring, until fragrant, about 3–4 minutes. add the meat and cook until it changes colour, about 3–4 minutes. cover and simmer for 15 minutes, then season to taste with salt. the mixture should be fairly dry, so if there's too much liquid, continue to simmer with the lid off.

TO ASSEMBLE: if you haven't seen the way they toss the dough in singapore, then just take it from me that this particular skill involves years of peeling **murtabaks** off the floor. trust me — go for the slightly less adventurous but high success rate of the following directions.

take a dough ball and place it on a smooth, flat surface, preferably a stainless steel bench top. *do not* flour the workbench or your hands. flatten the dough into a circle and, using your fingers, gradually spread the dough from the centre to the edges, until you have a circle about 30cm (12in) in diameter.

heat a griddle or a large cast-iron frying pan until very hot, grease it lightly with oil, and carefully place the dough in the centre. immediately brush the top of the dough with some beaten egg and place a sixth of the filling in the centre. fold over the dough so that each end overlaps the other a little. when the underside is golden, turn the murtabak carefully with a spatula and cook on the other side. remove carefully and drain on paper towels. repeat with the other five balls. serve while still warm.

variation: minced pork or beef — or even finely chopped vegetables — can be subsituted for the lamb. If you wish to serve **murtabak** as a dessert, try filling it with ripe, sliced bananas. Sprinkle sugar liberally over the top and finish with a swirl of condensed milk.

SINGAPORE NOODLES

Serves 4

3 tbsp dried shrimp
4 cups boiling water
500g (1 lb) rice flour
noodles or egg (hokkien)
noodles
3 tbsp vegetable oil
2 onions, finely sliced
2 tbsp all-purpose curry
powder
$^1/_2$ cup chicken stock
2 cloves garlic, chopped
100g (3$^1/_2$oz) small
uncooked prawns
200g (7oz) chao shao,
sliced into strips
(see glossary)
1 tbsp soy sauce
2 tbsp rice wine
2–3 spring onions
(scallions), sliced
diagonally
1 cup bean sprouts
salt and freshly ground
black pepper

Every country in Southeast Asia has its own noodle dish
— and I think Singapore's is the best. (Objectivity is not my forte!)
The only problem one encounters when ordering is that there is no
one such dish. Rather, the vendor will ask you to specify exactly
what kind of noodles you desire: hokkien, teochew or cantonese,
and will that be crispy or soft in a stir-fry or a broth?

soak the dried shrimp in 1 cup boiling water for 15 minutes; drain. soak the noodles in 3 cups boiling water for 5 minutes; drain. (if using fresh noodles, simply rinse and drain.) transfer the noodles to a large bowl.

heat half the oil in a wok and, when very hot, add the onions and shrimp and stir-fry for 2 minutes. stir in the curry powder and, when fragrant, add the stock. bring to the boil, then add to the noodles in the bowl and stir to coat.

pour the remaining oil into the wok, stir in the garlic and prawns and cook for a few minutes until pink. add the *chao shao* and soy sauce and stir-fry for 1 minute. stir in the rice wine and spring onions, then add to the noodles in the bowl along with the bean sprouts. toss the noodles, making sure they are well coated, and season to taste with salt and pepper. serve immediately.

[**note:** to make this a heartening soup, use 5–6 cups of stock.]

MUSSELS IN BLACK BEAN SAUCE

Serves 6

1.5kg (3lb) fresh black
mussels, scrubbed and
beards removed
5 tbsp vegetable oil
1 cup water
1 tbsp sesame oil
2.5cm (1in) piece ginger,
finely sliced
2 cloves garlic,
finely chopped
1$^1/_2$ tbsp black
bean paste
1 red pepper, cut into
5cm (2in) long strips
1 tbsp sherry
1 tsp sugar
1 tbsp soy sauce
1 tbsp cornflour mixed
with 1 cup water
$^1/_2$ bunch spring onions
(scallions), finely sliced

soak the mussels in a bowl of water for 30 minutes and drain well. heat 1 tablespoon vegetable oil in a wok or a wide, heavy-based saucepan with a lid. when hot, steam the mussels in 4 batches. place a quarter of the mussels in the bottom of the pan, cover with the lid and steam for 1 minute. shake the pan vigorously, pour in $^1/_4$ cup water, cover immediately and leave on the stove for a further minute. place the mussels in a bowl, discarding any that have not opened, and reserve the juices. repeat with the remaining mussles.

heat the sesame oil and the remaining tablespoon of vegetable oil in the wok. add the ginger, garlic, black bean paste and red pepper and stir-fry for 2 minutes. stir in the sherry, sugar, soy sauce and cornflour. return the mussels and their juices to the wok and allow the sauce to thicken slightly. toss in the spring onions and spoon into small serving bowls.

thailand

Thailand is an anomaly among its Southeast Asian neighbours. It is the only country that escaped colonisation by the profusion of imperial powers that used the entire region as their personal chessboard.

From the Dutch, Portuguese and British, to the French, German, American and Japanese,

Thailand has managed, through clever negotiation, timely choice of neutrality and 'acceptable' levels of foreign dominion, to do what every other nation has always fought for – retain its sovereignty.

The effect of this has filtered through to all aspects of Thai culture. As a result, Thai cuisine stands squarely on its own two feet. It is a true cuisine in the sense that it is complete – there is theory, continuity, balance and methodology. There is also a dish for every occasion. A growing number of connoisseurs (and opinionated gluttons such as myself) believe that Thai cookery rubs shoulders with the most highly esteemed cuisines of our time, namely French, Italian and Chinese. That is not to say that the kitchens of Thailand are devoid of influence. On the contrary, what they borrow from others they incorporate in such a way that it *becomes* quintessentially Thai.

Essential to an understanding of Thai cuisine is their use of contrast and balance. Hot, sweet, sour and salty are the four seasons of Thai cookery and they are blended with an exquisite understanding of complexity and intensity. Almost all individual dishes incorporate a mixture, while a meal itself will be a lesson in composed symmetry of these four seasons.

To explore Thai food one must start with the ingredients. The 'hot' element is most easily defined as the abundance of chillies. The Thais prefer the small, red bird-seye chilli with the hellfire touch. The literal translation of their nickname for these is 'devil's penis' – to be handled with extreme caution. The heat, however, also comes from the stacking of spices – the most common being coriander, cumin, turmeric and paprika – as well as freshly ground pepper and the generous use of ginger and garlic.

The 'sour' side of Thai cooking emanates from a multitude of unusual components.

There is the occasional use of vinegar, but it is the Thai's instinctive use of galangal that makes their method peerless in its scope. A more subtle version of ginger, galangal is widely used to give bite to soups and curries. Additionally, lemon grass, lime juice, kaffir lime leaves, pea eggplants and tamarind sluice the richness of many a dish and lift any stock beyond the realms of mere broth. At other times, to complement these ingredients, there is the inclusion of pandanus or betel leaves. Another fascinating aspect of Thai cuisine is their use of 'green' fruit, in particular unripe mangoes and pawpaw (papaya), that are tossed in a hot, sweet, sour and salty dressing to form the most startling side dish.

To counter the 'hot' there is the 'sweet' side of Thai cooking. Palm sugar is the most widely used and it has a distinctive slightly malty flavour, and, because of its unprocessed nature, it is not over-poweringly sweet. In between 'hot' and 'sweet' comes the seriously addictive sweet chilli sauce, which can be thrown into just about anything. Although many countries make a hot salsa, from the hot pepper sauce of the Caribbean to the much closer Korean cousin, *kimche*, none have the more-ishness nor the versatility of the Thai version. Add to this the Thais' extraordinary combination of tropical fruit in their sauces and salads, particularly curries that include pineapple and jackfruit, and the seemingly incongruous becomes symphonic.

The other notable balance to 'hot' and 'sour' is the use of coconut milk. The canned variety has freed many a Thai woman and child from countless hours of grinding and soaking the sweet flesh of the coconut, however there are those who refuse to bend to modern convenience and their cooking is all the more sensuous for it.

Last, but hardly least, is the salty 'season' of Thai cooking. Pungent shrimp paste and fish sauce provide flavour and fragrance to salads, salsas, soups, stir-fries and curries. There are squid and baby shrimp that are commonly used as a basis for stocks, as well as a very restrained use of soy sauce.

In homes and restaurants everywhere the most prized possession in the Thai kitchen is the mortar and pestle. There is a certain sanctity that comes with physically grinding the ingredients, and it is by far the most efficient method of prompting the ingredients to 'give up' their flavour. This is even more so when salt is added to the process, as it is a well-known catalyst for enticing the flavour-bound juices to exit their host.

Special mention should also be made of the herbs used in Thai cooking. The most common is coriander, otherwise known as cilantro or Chinese parsley. The Thais use it abundantly, both the roots, which are used in stock and curry pastes, and the leaves, which are retained for fresh salsas, salads and as garnish. Almost as popular is Thai basil or holy basil, a very aromatic herb with anise overtones, used in curries and most frequently stir-fries; and Vietnamese mint, which is actually from the buckwheat family and is ideal to finish off a dish rich in coconut milk.

When describing Thai cuisine, it is often the full-bodied flavours that hug the limelight. However, there is a great deal of subtlety that is overlooked. The gentle perfume of freshly steamed Jasmine rice for example, good enough to eat on its own and yet sympathetic to a whole range of uses, is but one of the incantations the Thai cook utilises to balance the wrath of a wicked curry.

North of the touristic overload of Chiang Mai, along the Mekong River in the east to Nong Khai, and towards Mae Hong Son and the Burmese (Myanmar) border in the west, is where the traditional cuisine of Northern Thailand can be found. The Thai government has always monitored the borders with all the vehemence of a territorial bloodhound – allowing very little trade through (except certain contraband deemed profitable to the local constabulary) and holding to an extremely hard line when it comes to refugees and mountain tribes. It is here in the villages of the foothills and river plains that the perpetuation of Thai culture and the subsistence nature of the Thai farmer is on display. The traditional savoury stick rice, which is rolled into balls in the fingers and dipped onto sauces that scream with flavour and chilli, is still a favourite. The 'jungle curries', as they are known, are thin and fiery without the addition of coconut milk and contain only those fish which survive the shadowy, lightning current of the border rivers.

It would be easy to continue singing the praises of this most remarkable country, but if truth be known, the Thais don't reach nirvana with everything they touch. One glaring example is the national drink – Thailand's answer to Draino – the lethal-by-name-, lethal-by-taste, Mekong rum. An all-purpose, paint-stripping degreaser, with anti-leech fortitude and the acidic finish of industrial varnish. Thankfully the Thais' reputation concentrates on its food!

Travelling south, one passes the old capitals of Sukhothai and Ayuthaya, serene epitaphs to the nation's former glory. West towards the Burmese border, on the imfamous River Kwai, there is a place called Kanchana Buri. It's a pretty settlement that shows no sign of the POW enslavement that raged here in the name of imperial desire. For me it is a special place; the burial ground of my grandfather. He lies, like thousands of others, in a well-maintained plot (fifth row back, ten along), as a tribute to the

senseless craft of war. The railway still operates along some of the very rafters he would have helped carry – and all for a bowl of plain rice per day that sustained him before he succumbed to dysentery. I remember gazing down at his bronze, cloned headstone, wondering what kind of person he was – I never met him, although he did write of the Thais and how, at the risk of their own lives, they helped supply many of the sick with food. The locals never challenged the Japanese, but by offering the occasional vegetables, particularly yams and a variety of fresh fruits, they helped sustain the sick and made all the difference in the world to those who did return.

Very few traces of this legacy can be found in the nation's capital, Bangkok, where high-rises and hectic traffic are punctuated by islands of serenity – the *wahs* (temples) and the incomparably gaudy royal palace – compass points that make it the penultimate 'east meets west' metropolis. It's a great pity that the fumes from the roaring *tuk-tuks* (three-wheeled, motorised rickshaws) and the two-stroke sports bikes have most visitors clutching handkerchiefs over their noses, because underneath all the pollution is the aroma of one of the great street food capitals of the world. Every turn reveals carts laden with fresh produce, stalls of beautifully carved fruit, roadside eateries shrouded in steaming cauldrons of soup and a parade of char-grills drowned in the smoky haze of barbecued *everything*.

The south of Thailand, with its abundance of seafood, coconut and tropical fruits (at times, all in one dish), reflects the climatic differences and regional influence that separates it from the north. Yet this incorporation of such flavours belies a greater understanding – a culinary sophistication – that continues to surprise and inspire all who visit. I will never forget the seafood curries of Ao Phra Nang, rich with coconut milk, blazing with chilli and sweet with pineapple, nor the stir-fried squid of Krabi.

Thai cuisine deserves a special place alongside those cultures whose culinary history is regarded as high art. It has depth (helped, no doubt, by an uninterrupted history), as well as a playfulness and resourcefulness that comes from being practised and redefined every minute of the day. The Thais are a nation of street-eaters, and generally consume just one main meal a day, surely a simple case of leaving plenty of room for the incredible range of roadside snacks: for street food is synonymous with the very existence of the Thai people.

1 tbsp vegetable oil
1 tsp shrimp paste
(see glossary)
3 cloves garlic, sliced
1 tsp palm sugar
1 spring onion (scallion)
cut into diagonal 1cm
(¹/₃in) lengths
4 cups fish stock or
water
¹/₂ cup tamarind water
(see glossary)
1 stalk lemon grass,
thinly sliced diagonally
5cm (2in) piece galangal,
sliced
3 kaffir lime leaves
2 tbsp chopped
coriander root
12 button mushrooms,
quartered
¹/₄ cup fish sauce
2 birdseye chillies, sliced
salt and white pepper
500g (1lb) uncooked
king prawns, peeled and
deveined, tails left on
and heads removed
a few thin slices of lime
1 spring onion (scallion),
sliced
some coriander leaves,
to garnish

TOM YUM GOONG
[hot and sour prawn soup]

This is probably the nearest thing there is to a national dish in Thailand. In Pratunam market, Bangkok, row upon row of soup stalls beckon to passers-by. The pace is furious, with fresh produce being whisked back and forth between table and kitchen, and customers coming and going in an almost time-lapse procession. No sooner do you sit down than a bowl of steaming **tom yum goong** *is thrust under your nose, assailing the senses.*

heat the vegetable oil in a large wok over high heat and fry the shrimp paste until fragrant, about 1 minute, stirring constantly. add the garlic, sugar and the chopped stem end of the spring onion, and stir-fry for 1 minute. pour in the stock or water, bring to the boil, then reduce heat to a gentle simmer. add the tamarind water, lemon grass, galangal, kaffir lime leaves, chopped coriander root, mushrooms, fish sauce and chillies, and simmer for 15 minutes. add the prawns and cook until they turn pink, about 2–3 minutes. check seasoning and remove from heat.

serve immediately, garnished with a slice of lime, some spring onion and a few sprigs of coriander leaves.

TOM YUM TALAY
[coconut seafood soup]

A 40-minute boat journey from the coastal town of Krabi and I was amongst the unbelievable beauty of Ao Phra Nang — a tied island approachable only by sea and surrounded by dripping limestone cliffs, emerald–azure water and pristine beaches. By mid-morning I was on my way to the local food stall, parked under palm fronds a dozen lazy steps from the water. The prize was their seafood soup, which was so good I couldn't stand the wait till lunch. There was just enough heat to repel any remaining drowsiness, which, in true Thai fashion, was perfectly countered by the sweet, tangy zip of pineapple.

carefully open the cans of coconut milk and skim off the thick 'cream' at the top — about 4 tablespoons. heat this cream in a heavy-based saucepan or large wok, add the shrimp paste and gently stir-fry until fragrant, about 2 minutes.

add the spring onion, red pepper, garlic and palm sugar and fry for a further 2 minutes. pour in the stock and bring to the boil, then add the remaining coconut milk and reduce heat to a simmer.

add all the remaining ingredients (except the pineapple and coriander leaves) and simmer until the seafood is cooked, about 5–8 minutes. remove from heat, stir in the pineapple chunks and garnish with coriander leaves. serve immediately.

2 x 400ml (14fl.oz) cans coconut milk (do not shake before opening)
1 tsp shrimp paste (see glossary)
1 spring onion (scallion), sliced diagonally into 1cm (1/3in) lengths
1 red pepper, cut into 2cm (3/4 in) long strips
2 cloves garlic, crushed
1 tsp palm sugar
500ml (16fl.oz) fish stock or water
4 tbsp fish sauce
1kg (2lb) mixed seafood — bite-sized chunks of white fish, scallops, uncooked prawns, mussels and strips of squid
1 stalk lemon grass, thinly sliced diagonally
5cm (2in) piece galangal, sliced
3 kaffir lime leaves
2 tbsp chopped coriander root
2 cups fresh pineapple chunks
coriander leaves, to garnish

200g (7oz) white-fleshed
fish fillets
2 tbsp salt
vegetable oil,
for deep-frying

YAM PLA FU
[crispy fish salad]

In Chang Khan, by the banks of the Mekong, an old woman and
her daughters worked methodically to prepare the **yam pla fu** *for the*
men returning from the fields. The regional staple of savoury
sticky rice was rolled into a ball, plunged into **nam prik** *(see recipe opposite)*
and followed by this delicious salad that could only be a product of the Thai
palate. As the fishing outriggers slipped past on the
treacherous current and the sun sank over the forbidden
banks of Laos, I felt a deep sadness for the great distance western
culture has put between us and the simplicity of existence
I experienced that afternoon.

rub the fish fillets with salt and grill, or roast in a medium oven, until cooked through. (cooking time will depend on the type and size of the fillet). allow to cool.

in a food processor or blender, process the fish in batches until it has the consistency of breadcrumbs. heat the oil in a wok until very hot. add a quarter of the fish mixture — it should puff up immediately. once it stops bubbling, gently turn the fish over and continue frying until golden brown. drain on paper towels and repeat with the remaining fish. serve with savoury sticky rice, **nam prik** and **som tam mamuang dip** (page 56).

[**note**: savoury sticky rice is not the same as the dessert sticky rice used on page 62. It is available from Asian food stores and should be cooked according to packet directions.]

NAM PRIK
[hot chilli sauce]

There are as many variations of this accompaniment as there are swear words for when you bite into a fiery chilli. The two most common are nam prik pla *(chilli fish sauce) and* nam prik kapi *(shrimp paste), but no matter what, they all contain enough heat to melt the Arctic icepack. There are very few eateries that do not provide a homemade* **nam prik** *— there were even some places to which I returned to eat only this with boiled rice!*

Makes about 1 cup

1 tbsp vegetable oil
4 cloves garlic, chopped
1 stalk lemon grass,
bruised and chopped
8 fresh red chillies,
chopped
1 tbsp freshly chopped
coriander root
1 tbsp shrimp paste
1 tbsp dried shrimp
2 tbsp palm sugar
$1/_4$ cup lime juice
$1/_4$ cup fish sauce
salt and white pepper
3–4 birdseye chillies
6 pea eggplants
coriander leaves

heat the oil and gently fry the garlic, lemon grass, chillies, coriander root and shrimp paste until fragrant. tip this mixture into a food processor or blender, add the dried shrimps and sugar, and blend to a paste, adding a little water to facilitate the process. place the paste in a bowl and whisk in the lime juice and fish sauce. taste for seasoning (be careful!) and garnish with whole birdseye chillies, pea eggplants and a few fresh coriander leaves.

4 very firm green
mangoes, julienned
2 handfuls bean sprouts
1 carrot, julienned
(optional)
1/4 bunch each whole
coriander and mint
leaves
**nam prik
taeng gwa** (below)

Makes about 2 cups

1 tbsp palm sugar
2 tbsp lime juice
2 tbsp water
1 clove garlic, chopped
2.5cm (1in) piece ginger,
chopped
2 red chillies, chopped
1 small cucumber,
seeded, peeled and sliced
1 spring onion (scallion),
sliced diagonally
1 tbsp chopped
coriander leaves
1 tbsp fish sauce
1 tbsp mint leaves,
chopped
100g (3 1/2 oz) roast
peanuts
salt and white pepper

SOM TAM MAMUANG DIP
[green mango salad]

This is a salad popular all over Thailand. The main ingredient varies depending on where you sample it — sometimes it's made with green pawpaw (papaya). **Som tam mamuang dip** *is as refreshing a salad as the imagination can conceive. By the river Kwai, under a sweltering sky (the same one my grandfather toiled under), I watched a Thai woman assemble it in minutes.*

place the ingredients in a bowl, toss with half the **nam prik taeng gwa**, spoon a little dressing on top as a garnish and serve immediately.

[**note:** make sure the mangoes are shiny and hard — if not the salad won't have the desired 'zing'.]

NAM PRIK TAENG GWA
[chilli cucumber and roast peanut dressing]

dissolve the sugar in the lime juice and water, stir in the remaining ingredients and season to taste with salt and pepper.

GAI YANG NAM JIM GAI WAN

[char-grilled sweet chilli chicken]

Serves 6

Here it is, the perennial favourite of the backpacker, though the Thais love this as much as any traveller. It is possible to buy sweet chilli sauce in most supermarkets and it need not be reserved only for chicken — try it with squid or octopus. However, for the best results use homemade sweet chilli sauce— it makes all the difference.

make a few cuts down to the bone on each side of the drumsticks.

MARINADE: place the marinade ingredients in a food processor or blender and blend to a paste. rub the marinade over the chicken and leave to marinate overnight in the refrigerator.

SWEET CHILLI SAUCE: place the sugar and vinegar in a small saucepan and dissolve the sugar over low heat. cook until the liquid is reduced by a quarter. remove from heat and add the garlic and chillies; stir well and allow to cool. add the coriander leaves and season to taste with salt.

grill the chicken over low heat on a barbecue or in a char-grill pan, turning constantly and basting with the marinade. cook until just done, about 10 minutes. brush with the sweet chilli sauce and serve with a bowl of the sweet chilli sauce for people to help themselves.

6 free-range chicken drumsticks

MARINADE
4 cloves garlic, chopped
5cm (2in) piece ginger, grated
1 tsp salt
1 tsp white peppercorns
1/2 bunch coriander
1 tsp palm sugar
3 tbsp fish sauce

SWEET CHILLI SAUCE
1 cup palm sugar
1 cup white vinegar
4 cloves garlic, finely chopped
12 fresh red chillies, seeded and finely chopped
1/2 bunch coriander leaves, finely chopped
salt

500g (1lb) flat rice
noodles
1 tbsp sesame oil
1 tbsp sesame seeds
1 tbsp rice wine vinegar
2 tbsp soy sauce
1 tbsp vegetable oil
2 cloves garlic, crushed
1 cup coconut cream
1/4 cup peanut butter
1 tbsp fish sauce
salt and white pepper
1/4 cup chopped spring
onions (scallions)
2 tbsp crushed roasted
peanuts

SESAME PEANUT NOODLES

*I don't know the correct name for this dish but I have a sneaking
feeling it was one man's domain. The flock of customers to this most
unassuming slurp-fest was all the proof I needed to try out
the noodles and attempt to recreate them.*

cook the noodles in a pot of boiling, salted water according to packet directions; drain. combine the sesame oil, sesame seeds, vinegar and soy sauce in a large bowl. add the noodles and toss to coat. cover and keep warm.

heat the vegetable oil in a frying pan and gently fry the garlic for 1 minute. add the coconut cream and peanut butter and stir for 2–3 minutes. remove from heat, stir in the fish sauce and season to taste with salt and pepper.

to serve, place some noodles in a serving bowl, top with a generous spoonful of the sauce and sprinkle with spring onions and crushed peanuts.

Serves 4

6 cloves garlic
5cm (2in) piece ginger
4 red chillies
1 stalk lemon grass
1 kaffir lime leaf
1 bunch coriander roots
2 tbsp vegetable oil
500g (1lb) squid,
cleaned, diagonally
scored and cut into 5cm
(2in) x 1cm (1/3in)
lengths
2 banana chillies or
1 yellow pepper, sliced
2 tbsp fish sauce
1 tbsp palm sugar
1 small bunch thai basil
salt and white pepper

PLA MEUK PAT PRIK
[spicy stir-fried squid]

*A popular method used throughout Thailand for stir-frying just
about anything — squid, thin strips of meat, chicken and
for vegetarians, mushrooms or green beans.*

roughly chop the garlic, ginger, red chillies, lemon grass, kaffir lime leaf and coriander roots. place in a food processor or blender and blend to a paste.

heat the oil in a wok and stir-fry the paste until fragrant, about 2 minutes. add the squid and banana chillies or yellow pepper and stir-fry for 2 minutes.

add the remaining ingredients and stir-fry for 1 minute. season to taste with salt and pepper and serve immediately.

MIANG GUNG
[prawns wrapped in betel leaves]

Serves 6

heat the oil in a saucepan and lightly fry the garlic, lemon grass and shrimp paste. add the fish sauce and palm sugar and simmer for a few minutes. transfer to a mixing bowl and toss with the prawns, chillies and toasted coconut.

lay out the betel or banana leaves or foil and place on some ginger, a slice of lime and a spoonful of the prawn mixture. top with some crushed peanuts and coriander leaves. wrap into a neat parcel, secure with a toothpick (if using leaves) and steam for about 15 minutes. serve hot or cold.

1 tbsp vegetable oil
2 cloves garlic, crushed
1 stalk lemon grass,
finely sliced
1 tsp shrimp paste
(see glossary)
1/4 cup fish sauce
1 tbsp palm sugar
150g (5oz) small
uncooked prawns,
peeled and deveined
2 red chillies, seeded and
finely chopped
3 tbsp shredded coconut,
toasted (see glossary)
12 betel leaves
(see glossary)
or banana leaves or foil
2.5cm (1in) piece ginger,
julienned
2 limes, thinly sliced
12 tbsp crushed roasted
peanuts
1/2 bunch coriander leaves

2 x 400ml (14fl.oz) cans
coconut milk (do not
shake before opening)
800ml (24fl.oz) chicken
stock or water
1/4 cup fish sauce
2 kaffir lime leaves
5cm (2in) piece galangal,
sliced
1kg (2lb) chicken breasts,
cut into bite-sized pieces
1 cup chopped pumpkin
1 red pepper, sliced
6 thai basil leaves
juice of 1 lime
salt and black pepper
coriander leaves

PASTE
1 tbsp vegetable oil
2 tsp coriander seeds
1 tsp ground cumin
1 tsp shrimp paste
1 tsp white peppercorns
1 tsp salt
4 cloves garlic, crushed
5cm (2in) piece ginger,
sliced
2 spring onions
(scallions), chopped
1 tbsp palm sugar
1 stalk lemon grass, sliced
6 green chillies, seeded
and chopped
1 bunch coriander, roots
chopped

GAENG KIEW WAN GAI
[green chicken curry]

The Thai New Year, Songkran, is celebrated in April and is a festival of much mischief. My friend and I went to one of the more civilised restaurants in Ao Phra Nang, just a few short steps from the gently lapping seashore, and proceeded to waterbomb the patrons, attracting many an evil stare. However, it wasn't long until this reviously serene establishment degenerated into a theme park of flying water and screaming kids. Drenched and breathless, we took refuge at a quiet corner table and consumed the most delicious green curry while the saturation we had started continued unabated.

to make the paste, heat the vegetable oil in a wok and gently fry the coriander seeds and cumin until fragrant, about 2 minutes. place in a food processor or blender with the remaining paste ingredients and blend to a smooth paste.

carefully open the cans of coconut milk and skim the thick 'cream' from the top — about 4 tablespoons — reserve coconut milk. heat this cream in a heavy-based saucepan, add the curry paste and cook, stirring, until fragrant and well incorporated, about 5 minutes. pour in the remaining coconut milk and the equivalent amount of stock or water. add the fish sauce, lime leaves, galangal, chicken, pumpkin, red pepper and thai basil and simmer until the chicken is just cooked, about 15–20 minutes. remove from heat, stir in half the lime juice and season to taste with salt and pepper.

serve topped with fresh coriander leaves and accompanied by steamed jasmine rice.

variation: this is an ideal dish to make vegetarian, as many thais do. simply substitute tofu or vegetables for the chicken and shorten the cooking time. mushrooms, green beans and broccoli make ideal additions and, if really strict, you can omit the shrimp paste and/or fish sauce without losing too much flavour.

note: there are commercially prepared curry pastes on the market which, if you're pushed for time, are a good alternative to preparing your own paste. The end result is still delicious, especially if used in conjunction with fresh kaffir lime leaves, galangal, thai basil and coriander. try to purchase curry paste imported from thailand, and use 1–2 tablespoons, depending on personal taste, fry in coconut cream as you would for the homemade paste, and continue cooking as above.

GAENG PHET
[red beef curry]

One of the beauties of Thai cuisine is that almost all the food
prepared in restaurants is also available from street-side vendors.
In Ayathaya, a night market was set up by the banks of the
Chao Phraya River, where row upon row of heavenly-scented curries
were displayed to tease (and eventually defeat) the appetite.
This dish is a Thai classic.

to make the paste, heat the vegetable oil in a wok and gently fry the coriander seeds and cumin until fragrant, about 2 minutes. place in a food processor or blender with the remaining paste ingredients and blend to a smooth paste.

carefully open the cans of coconut milk and skim the thick 'cream' from the top — about 4 tablespoons — reserve the milk. heat this cream in a heavy-based saucepan, add the curry paste and cook, stirring, until fragrant and well incorporated, about 5 minutes. pour in the remaining coconut milk and the equivalent amount of stock or water. add a splash of fish sauce, the kaffir lime leaves, galangal, beef and thai basil, and simmer until the beef is very tender, about 50–60 minutes. add the green beans 5 minutes before the end of cooking time. remove from heat and season to taste with salt and pepper. stir through the lime juice and sesame oil, garnish with fresh coriander leaves and serve with steamed jasmine rice.

variation: to make this dish vegetarian, substitute 2 large eggplants, cubed, for the beef. cook gently until very tender, about 15 minutes.

[
note: there are commercially prepared curry pastes on the market which, if you're pushed for time, are a good alternative to preparing your own paste. The end result is still delicious, especially if used in conjunction with fresh kaffir lime leaves, galangal, thai basil and coriander. try to purchase curry paste imported from thailand, and use 1–2 tablespoons, depending on personal taste. fry in coconut cream as you would for the homemade paste, and continue cooking as above.
]

Serves 6

2 x 400ml (14fl.oz) cans coconut milk (do not shake before opening)
800ml (24fl.oz) beef stock or water
splash of fish sauce
2 kaffir lime leaves
5cm (2in) piece galangal, sliced
1kg (2lb) beef, preferably rump or blade, cut into bite-sized pieces
6 thai basil leaves
1 cup chopped green beans
salt and white pepper
juice of 1 lime
2 tsp sesame oil

PASTE
1 tbsp vegetable oil
2 tsp coriander seeds
1 tsp ground cumin
1 tsp shrimp paste
1 tsp white peppercorns
1 tsp salt
4 cloves garlic, crushed
5cm (2in) piece ginger, chopped
2 spring onions (scallions), chopped
1 tbsp palm sugar
1 stalk lemon grass, sliced
6 fresh red chillies, seeded and chopped
coriander leaves, to garnish

KIAOW NIAOW MAMUANG
[mango with sticky rice]

*2 cups sticky rice (the
short-grained, pearly
white variety), soaked
overnight in 4 cups
water
3 cups coconut cream
$1/2$ tsp salt
$1^1/2$ cups palm sugar
1 cinnamon stick or 2
split cardamom pods or
freshly grated nutmeg or
1 pandanus leaf
(optional)
4–5 large banana or
pandanus leaves (see
glossary), cut into 30cm
(12in) squares
2 large mangoes, sliced*

*Wrapped in banana or pandanus leaves, these parcels are reason
enough to visit Thailand. My breakfast ritual in Bangkok consisted of
purchasing one of these little bundles and making my way to a
wat (temple) — those islands of serenity in the midst of all the
chaotic traffic. This dish is simplicity itself, yet nothing quite grabs
me the same way as peeling back the leaves and luxuriating in the aroma.*

rinse the rice thoroughly and drain well. place the rice in a heavy-based saucepan with enough water to cover by 2.5cm (1in) and 'steam' on low heat until the grains are soft, about 20 minutes.

put the coconut cream, salt, sugar and choice of flavouring (if desired) in an enamel saucepan (this stops the coconut cream discolouring), and cook, stirring constantly, over low heat for 10–15 minutes.

put the rice in a glass bowl, pour over the coconut cream mixture, stir and allow to steep for about 1 hour. once cool, place 3 heaped tablespoons of the mixture in the centre of each banana leaf square and top with a few slices of mango. fold over the flaps and secure with a toothpick. serve soon after assembling.

india & nepal

If there is one word that best describes India, it would have to be **intense**. No other country contains such myriad contradictions within its own fabric – a weft and weave that is as colourful as it is intricate – blending a tumultuous history with an unforgiving climate and a population bulging towards one billion.

Not so much a country as a loose confederation, the Indian subcontinent is divided into sixteen diverse regions and boats several hundred dialects – the very reason why communication across state boundaries is almost always conducted in English. To add to the complexity of the equation, India is a country where 85 per cent of the people are Hindu *and* it's the second largest Muslim nation on earth. Anywhere else in the world, minorities of such size are a recipe for chaos. Yet India embraces the mania of its predicament in an attempt to forge a nation of tolerance and acceptance. Along with this diversity of peoples and tongues comes a cuisine of great regional specialities.

Indian people care about their food like no other country I have visited. Food is creation – and the preparation of food a form of personal expression and respect. A proper understanding of food goes beyond the physical side of cooking and eating, for it is the connection point of human spirit and earthy soul. Food is an unmistakable part of the Indian culture.

Specific dishes and produce are interlaced with religious festivities and rites of passage, and form an intricate part of the social system. In fact, no Indian cook would prepare a meal without great consideration for whom the meal is for – their age, likes, and dislikes, the time of eating and the climate. They take into account which ingredients are in season, the balance of flavours (salty, spicy, sour and sweet) and textures (soft, crispy, wet and dry) as well as the order and timing of all these factors. Consequently, the street food of India has inherited a special place in the nation's psyche. People can rely on certain foods always being available outside their local temple or, on particular days of worship, there will always be *puri thali* (fried bread and condiments) at every train stop, **samousas** at every bus station and **chai** just about anywhere at any time.

Traditional Hindu cuisine in its purest form is totally vegetarian. One of their strongest beliefs, which they share with Buddhists, is in not harming any living being – and in India there is no higher being than the Brahmin cow. To witness the absolute right of way which these animals have, and the privileges bestowed upon them, is something that would drop the jaw of any cattle-hardened jackeroo. It has been suggested that much of this has to do with the culture of poverty as it does religion. In a country where resources are short, arable land diminishing and the population immense, a vegetarian existence is a way of ensuring sustainable existence.

A live Brahmin cow not only brings milk and its by-products, yoghurt and cheese, but also the holiest of holies in Indian cuisine, clarified butter or ghee. Like all products of the cow, ghee is considered a purifier (as is dried cow dung, which is used to full effect, either as fuel for fires, or by pulverising, mixing with water and spreading out as flooring or pavement in and around rural homes). Even in Muslim households, ghee is regarded as a sign of prosperity – a status symbol. To sport a generous girth from the overindulgence

of ghee is proof that one's business is looked favourably upon by the gods. As one zest-infested merchant said while stroking his potbelly, 'Health means wealth!'.

While I have endeavoured to offer recipes from right across India, the majority come from the south where I spent most of my time. Here strict Hindu philosophy still holds court over many aspects of daily existence – right down to the correct etiquette of presentation. Snacks, or *tiffin*, occupy an almost sacred place in the every day. *Wallahs* juggling stacks of silver *tiffin* containers that sway atop their rickety bicycles, glide nonchalantly through the chaotic bazaars. Each stack comes with strict markings that dictate exactly where they are going and to whom. The precision seems almost supernatural ... and very Indian, for there is most definitely a method in their madness.

The alternative to *tiffin* is the highly economic, fiery mystery of 'rice and meals' – a sort of chef's special of the day, offering an assortment of **dhal**, *subzi* (vegetable stew), **raita** (a yoghurt and cucumber condiment) and *puri* (fried wholemeal bread). Like most of the locals, I would sit down to 'meals' once a day and enjoy *tiffin* whenever I was in the need for a top up – or whenever my curiosity got the better of me.

The south of India is rice-and-dhal country. It's where a more simplistic existence is pursued and people always use the *right* hand – 'the natural spoon of life'. Here the lifestyle is more rural in essence, and is reflected in the awareness of the seasons, the adherence to traditional days of feasts and facts, and in the celebrations that mark the harvest, weddings and religious festivals.

Mysore, with its grand palaces, unparalleled spice market and air hazy with the scent of freshly lathered sandalwood, is a centre for southern produce. It bustles with furious activity, and one can witness the process of life: the cotton carts that limp into town, the stained sidewalks outside the dyeing factories, the many cloth shops selling 'suiting and shirting' where you can purchase the fabric of your choice, walk around the corner to the street-side tailors who will measure you on the spot and produce a tailor-fitted suit by the afternoon.

Further south is the tropical paradise of Kerala, where bananas, coconuts and seafood reign supreme. Here, too, there are huge harvests of mango and jackfruit, curries made with every kind of sea morsel, and a tearaway destruction of the monsoonal season. The southern tip of India, Tamil Nadu, is different again with the influence of Sri Lankan spice and the famous fiery curries of Madras.

At the top of the east coast lies Calcutta, a city of tremendous paradox and hideous extremes. A place where rickshaw *wallahs* still pull beautifully attired women in saris through streets littered with beggars. Yet somehow in the mayhem of humanity, Calcutta emerges as a city of hope. It also boats some of the most unusual street food on the subcontinent, enhanced by the unmistakable touch the Bengali sweetmaker. A particularly seductive find was the warm buffalo milk, infused with cardamom seeds and sweetened with sugar – a welcome nightcap to anyone with just a few rupees to spare.

The contrast between northern and southern India, and in particular the Islamic and Hindu religions, is wonderfully displayed in the meat markets of Delhi. My travelling partner at the time loves to recount the sheer brutal delight that one Muslim butcher wrought from his chopping board. 'See this?' he would say pointing at a slab of meat, while casting a malevolent eye at the Hindus. 'This, my friend, is COW!' and down would come the cleaver. A deep and evil belly laugh would follow.

It is in the north of the country that the dominion of the Mughal, Arabic and Persian influence becomes predominant. Mughali cuisine is indeed synonymous with any auspicious occasion, for they brought opulence, grandeur and extravagance to the subcontinent and a cuisine rich with nuts, dried fruits and meats of every description. All this combined to develop into the specialities of **biriyanis** and *pillaos*, kebabs and curries thickened with ground almonds, cashews and cream, and of course tandoor cuisine. Perhaps the most widespread influence came with the introduction of flour, for Indian bread in all its delicious diversity, whether it be the stuffed *naan* of Hyderabad or the homeground *chapati* of the peasant farmer, is among the greatest of the country's culinary achievements.

If searching for refinement, inventiveness and subtlety in Indian cuisine, **palak** is the supreme example: a delicious combination of mild spices and pureed spinach that forms the basis for a dish that can feature any one of a number of combinations. **Palak paneer** has melt-in-the-mouth homemade fresh cheese, **aloo palak** has spiced potatoes, and then there are the pairings with meat, particularly lamb and beef. Although there are variations across the continent, it is a dish that originates in the Punjab – the Sikhs are a proud race (everyone carries the surname Singh, meaning lion) who refuse to be aligned with the Hindu crush. Indeed their distinctive turbans, well-manicured features and air of dignity, affords them a unique place amongst the masses.

Dotted throughout India there are the unusual outposts – high-tide marks of previous imperial decadence – such as the British hill stations in Jammu, Kashmir, Darjeeling and Kodaikanal, and the Portuguese enclave of Goa. In Goa the cuisine is sublime, combining the cooking methods of the Portuguese with the rich spice of central India, and rounded out with the creaminess of coconut, it was here, with the very Indian Pereira family, that I dined on shark curry and stuffed squid, and drank the liquid nitrate known as *fenni*, fermented from coconut. And all served in a palm-shaded café, overlooking golden sands where brazenly colourful women from Karnataka smiled tirelessly as they try to sell their exquisite home-spun cloth. Here, too, you will find the saffron merchants plying their wares up and down the beach and looking awkwardly out of place in suit, tie and briefcase.

There are some ingredients that are common to all aspects of Indian cuisine, and as such have earned a very special status as either medicinally beneficial or religiously pious. Garlic is the magic cureall especially favoured for circulatory and respiratory ailments. Yoghurt is a digestive aid, crucial to cooling down the system between bouts of hell-fire curries. Ginger and turmeric are the purifiers of the system and valued for their antiseptic qualities, while ghee, as already mentioned, is the lubricator of the wellbeing.

In Nepal, the diet shows a greater resemblance to the food of southern India than the food of the north with which it shares a border. The national dish, known as *dhal baht* (dhal and rice) is indicative of the severe lack of fresh produce available in the mountain villages. The most interesting influence has come from the influx of Tibetan culture that has occurred since the Chinese invasion of their motherland. The continued persecution of Tibetans in their own land has only led to their culture being more closely adhered to while in exile. Although the Tibetan capital in exile, Dharmastala – home of the Tibetan spiritual leader, the Dalai

Lama – is, in fact, in the north of India, many refugees have settled in the high plains of Nepal. It is at times a very cruel and brutal existence, yet the similarity between the landscape here and their own homeland affords the Tibetan people some respite in their plight.

Nepalese cuisine is limited by the very nature of what makes the country so physically stunning – the picturesque and barely arable Himalaya. Yet the people still pursue a creative approach in turning such land to sustainable use. The diligence of the Nepalese in creating steppes on such slopes is astonishing. On such mountainous terrain, every flat surface is used for either growing or dying or both. Consequently, flat roofs have a special purpose, particularly in close-knit villages where one person's roof is their neighbours drying and sorting space. Within such limitations, resourcefulness is born – the people of Nepal have managed to turn the most mundane of raw produce into food of substantial and tasty design.

Kathmandu Valley is as beautiful as it is treacherous. Lush to the point of almost being tropical, yet embraced by the forearms of the snow-capped Himalaya. The frenzied heart of the Nepalese capital is Darmar Square, a marketplace of bruised fruit, grubby vegetables and the stench of dried fish that have come from god-knows-where. Amongst the rickshaws cranked by human feet, money-changers and the haggling masses, are the bone-spider children, darting between the horn-manic traffic. Here, too, are temples, squeezed vice-like into this chaos, with their magnificent wooden facades and intricate carvings that preach a world of ecstatic reincarnation and nightmare violence.

The Annapurna ranges are some of the most spectacular in the entire Himalayas. It is possible on a fairly well-trodden trail, to ascend one side of the range, make a pass of 5300 metres and return via the other side. The entire trek took me eighteen days and rates as one of the most mind-blowing experiences I have ever had. Cuisine on the way was sparse, and after leaving Pokhara, the only means of receiving supplies was by down-trodden donkey or the equally overloaded sherpas - Nepalese porters. These men worked continually on the nasty side of the pain barrier. Their unrecognisable, reptilian-like feet paid homage to the sheer weight of their occupational hazard. The sherpas lived day in, day out on *dahl baht* – plain rice, spinach dahl and often spiced potato. Perhaps not a varied diet, but one that has sustained their existence for centuries.

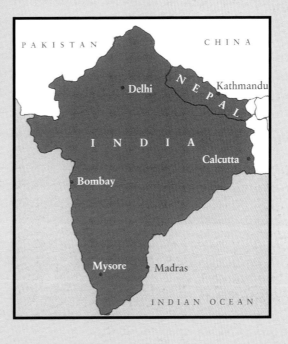

ALOO MATTAR SAMOUSA
[spiced potato and pea pastries]

In a thousand muddy depots across the Indian subcontinent,

buses as old as Adam line up to do battle with the rubble that passes

for roads. Drivers rev their engines, spitting diesel fumes into the stratosphere

and creating an air of insatiable panic. Into the writhing throng we passed,

doing battle with fellow passengers for the closest thing to a miracle on

public transport — a seat. Trays were pushed up against the windows

and a tea towel flicked back to reveal a batch of perfect **samousas.**

The dipping sauce was tangy, fiery and sweet all at once.

As we passed the creator of these marvels, gently swirling oil over

another batch, we showed him the **samousas.** *He nodded knowingly*

— the single serene being amongst all this chaos — and continued to craft

his wares as if it were a skill bestowed upon him by the gods.

DOUGH

2 cups plain flour

$^1/_2$ tsp salt

4 tbsp ghee, softened

$^1/_2$ cup iced water

(approximately)

FILLING

2 tbsp black mustard
seeds

1 tbsp ghee

1 tsp ground turmeric

1 tsp garam masala

2.5cm (1in) piece ginger,
very finely chopped

6 medium potatoes,
boiled, peeled and cut
into 1cm ($^1/_3$in) cubes

1 cup peas, steamed

salt

vegetable oil,
for deep-frying

DOUGH: sift the flour and salt into a bowl and rub in the softened ghee until the mixture is the consistency of breadcrumbs. add enough iced water to form a smooth ball and knead on a floured surface until the dough is elastic, about 10 minutes. cover with plastic wrap and allow to rest for 1 hour.

FILLING: put the mustard seeds into a frying pan over low heat. once they start popping, add the ghee, turmeric, garam masala and ginger and cook, stirring, until fragrant, about 2–3 minutes. stir in the potatoes to coat. remove from heat, mix in the peas, add salt to taste and set aside.

TO ASSEMBLE: roll the dough into a log and cut into 15 equal portions. roll out each portion until approximately 15cm (6in) in diameter and cut in half. moisten half the straight edge of the semi-circle and fold the dough over to form a cone shape. pinch the the straight edges together, making a 5mm ($^1/_4$in) seam. spoon in the filling until three-quarters full, moisten with water and pinch the top closed. make sure all seals are secure.

when ready, deep-fry the samousas in batches until golden, about 3–4 minutes, turning several times. drain on paper towels. serve with **imli chatni** (see opposite) or **raita** (page 73) on the side.

IMLI CHATNI
[tamarind chutney]

combine the ingredients in a bowl and stir until the sugar is dissolved.

serve with **samousas**.

Makes about 1 cup

*1/2 cup tamarind water
(see glossary)*
1 tbsp brown sugar
1 knob ginger, grated
1 clove garlic, crushed
1 tbsp lemon juice
*1 tbsp finely chopped
coriander*
1 tsp ground cumin
*1 birdseye chilli, finely
chopped*
salt, to taste

CHANNA DHAL
[chickpea dip]

Channa dhal, *sometimes referred to as butter dhal, is an almost-creamy, textured puree made with small, yellow split peas. It is invariably finished with onions sweated in ghee, garam masala and black mustard seeds. The most delicious bread to eat this with, for it must be eaten with the hands, is the flaky, slightly buttery* **paratha.**

soak the chickpeas or split peas overnight in water to cover (there is no need to soak red lentils). the next day, wash and rinse the pulse and place them in a large saucepan with the water, salt, ginger, turmeric and 1 tablespoon ghee. bring to the boil, then reduce heat and simmer until the **dhal** is almost of puree consistency, about 1^1/$_2$ hours for the chickpeas or split peas; 40–50 minutes for the red lentils.

melt the remaining ghee in a frying pan, add the onions and garlic and cook on a very low heat until they are opaque, about 3–4 minutes. stir in the coriander and mustard seeds. when the seeds begin to pop, add the garam masala and continue stirring for a few minutes until fragrant. immediately pour the contents of the frying pan into the **dhal** and stir through. serve with a squeeze of lemon and a sprinkle of chopped coriander leaves.

Serves 6–8

*2 cups dried yellow
chickpeas or red lentils or
yellow split peas*
8 cups water
2 tbsp salt, or to taste
*10cm (4in) piece ginger,
grated*
1 tsp ground turmeric
^{1}/$_2$ cup ghee
2 onions, diced
3 cloves garlic, crushed
1 tsp ground coriander
*2 tbsp black or brown
mustard seeds*
2 tsp garam masala
*1 lemon, plus extra
wedges to serve*
*^{1}/$_2$ cup chopped coriander
leaves*

3 cups atta or plain flour
$^{1}/_{2}$ tbsp baking powder
1 tsp salt, or to taste
$^{1}/_{2}$ tsp sugar
$^{1}/_{4}$ cup melted ghee, plus
$^{1}/_{4}$ cup extra
1 cup warm water
(approximately)
vegetable oil, for frying

PARATHA
[flaky bread]

There are chapatis, *a wholemeal flatbread;* puris, *a smaller,
deep-fried bread that puffs up and which seems the most popular
snack at two-minute train stops; and then somewhere between a
buttery-soft flatbread and a savoury croissant lies the flirtatious*
paratha. *Layers pull away in wisps from the centre of the bread
and almost melt as they scoop hot* **dhal** *to your lips.*

sift the flour and baking powder into a bowl and mix in the salt and sugar. rub in the melted ghee until the mixture is the consistency of breadcrumbs. pour in enough water to form a stiff dough. on a lightly floured surface, knead the dough until smooth, about 10–15 minutes. roll into a ball, rub all over with the extra melted ghee, cover with plastic wrap and allow to stand at room temperature for 2–3 hours.

knead the dough again for 2 minutes, then roll into a log and cut into 8 equal portions. roll each portion into a circle approximately 15cm (6in) in diameter. brush with ghee, fold in half and then fold again in the same direction. brush once more with ghee then turn the dough so it is vertical. Roll up the dough from the bottom to the top to form a short, fat 'cigar'. stand this on its end and push down to form a patty. roll out again to form a circle approximately 15cm (6in) in diameter, sprinkle with flour and set aside until all are complete.

cover the base of a crepe pan or wide, heavy-based frying pan with a thin film of oil and warm on low heat for 1 minute. fry each **paratha** gently, using a spatula to push the bread down to ensure the inside is cooking as well. cook for 3–4 minutes on each side. when the outside is golden and just beginning to crisp, remove and drain on paper towels. serve while warm.

[**note:** for the sweet tooth — and if there's any left over! — I suggest a squeeze of lemon over the top and a fine sprinkling of sugar.]

MASALA DOSA
[crisp pancakes with spiced potato filling]

Serves 8–10

In the crushed velvet interior of formerly British dining halls, waiters

in cement-starched uniforms offer trays of **masala dosa** *to those who*

have tired (and can afford it) of the chaotic Indian streets. In such

Raj-like settings under lopsided ceiling fans, I have eaten this dish

— as I have on the streets with nothing but a banana leaf

to support such refinement.

BATTER: drain the *urad dhal* and blend in a food processor or blender, adding water as necessary to make a thick paste. repeat this process with the rice and combine the rice and dhal with salt to taste. set aside overnight to ferment slightly, as this adds piquancy to their flavour.

FILLING: heat the ghee and fry the mustard and fenugreek seeds until they pop. stir in the onions, spices and ginger and cook until the onions are soft, taking care not to burn the spices. add the potatoes, stir to coat thoroughly and add water. cover and cook on low heat until all the water is absorbed, about 5 minutes. add salt to taste.

TO ASSEMBLE: heat a large cast-iron frying pan (when water drops sizzle, it is ready), and smear with a little oil. pour a small ladleful of batter into the centre and, using the back of the spoon, spread the batter in a circular, outward motion until about 30cm (12in) in diameter and paper-thin. pour a little oil around the edges and cook until the bottom of the **dosa** is lightly golden. transfer to a serving plate, spoon a few tablespoons of filling into the centre and fold to form in half. repeat with remaining mixture.

serve with **nariyal chatni** (page 72) and **sambar** (page 74).

BATTER
1 *cup* urad dhal *(husked black lentils), rinsed and soaked overnight in*
2 *cups water*
3 *cups parboiled rice, soaked overnight in*
6 *cups water*
1 *cup water*
salt
vegetable oil, for frying

FILLING
2 *tbsp ghee*
1 *tbsp brown mustard seeds*
1 *tbsp fenugreek seeds*
2 *onions, finely sliced*
1 *tsp ground turmeric*
1 *tsp garam masala*
1 *tsp* asafoetida *(see glossary)*
2cm (^{3}/$_4$in) *piece ginger, grated*
6 *medium potatoes, boiled, peeled and roughly chopped*
^{1}/$_2$ *cup water*
salt, to taste

vegetable oil

2.5cm (1in) piece ginger,
chopped
1 tsp tamarind water
(see glossary)
2 tbsp water
1/2 cup freshly grated
coconut or toasted,
shredded coconut, plus
extra to garnish
1 bunch coriander,
leaves only
4–6 green chillies,
chopped
salt, to taste
2 tbsp yoghurt (optional)

Serves 4

4 bunches english
spinach, leaves only
1/2 bunch coriander
2 tbsp vegetable oil
1 tbsp coriander seeds
1 tbsp cumin seeds
1 onion, finely sliced
2 cloves garlic, crushed
5cm (2in) piece ginger,
grated
2 green chillies, chopped
salt
500g (1lb) fresh cheese,
cut into 2cm (3/4in)
cubes (the closest
approximation would be
ricotta, however the
cheese is meant to stay
together, so a more
plausible alternative is
bocconcini)
4 red chillies, to garnish

NARIYAL CHATNI
[coconut chutney]

*A refreshing and fiery accompaniment to most of
southern India's tiffin.*

place the ginger, tamarind water and water in a food processor or blender and blend to
a paste. add the remaining ingredients and pulse until well incorporated but still a little
chunky. stir in yoghurt, if desired, and top with fresh or toasted coconut.

PALAK PANEER
[spiced spinach puree with fresh cheese]

*Just to prove that not all Indian dishes are overwhelmingly spicy,
here is a recipe for a simple dish: soft curd cheese floating in a velvet
spinach puree. Of all the flavours of India, it is* **palak paneer** *that
I most fondly remember.*

wash the spinach leaves, place in a large saucepan over medium heat and stir until
wilted. plunge immediately into icy cold water — this helps retain the vibrant colour.
puree the spinach and coriander leaves in a food processor or blender and scrape in to
a separate bowl.

heat the oil and fry the coriander and cumin seeds until fragrant, about 2 minutes. add
the onion, garlic, ginger and chillies and cook until the onion is translucent, about 3
minutes. remove from heat and allow to cool. puree in the food processor, add the
spinach mixture and pulse until all is well incorporated.

when ready to serve, transfer the puree to a saucepan, season to taste with salt, add the
cheese and gently warm through — you can thin it out with a little water, yoghurt or
coconut cream if desired. pour into serving bowls, garnish with a fresh red chilli and serve
with **paratha** (page 70).

VENGAYA PAKORA
[onion fritters]

*As popular as the **samousa**, **pakoras** are a type of vegetable fritter.*
This description, however, does no justice to the remarkable change
that takes place to simple vegetables once dipped in the nutty chickpea
batter. The most common version, in part because of its
*low cost, is the **vengaya pakora**. Although any vegetable can be*
substituted, the slightly acidic sweetness of onions perfectly
compliments the spicy coating.

BATTER: mix the ghee and the baking soda until foaming. combine the *besan* with the spices and salt, and add the ghee mixture. stir in the water, a little at a time, until a thick batter forms.

stir the filling ingredients into the batter.

TO ASSEMBLE: pour the oil into a heavy-based saucepan until it is about 5cm (2in) deep and heat until just smoking. gently drop heaped tablespoons of batter into the hot oil, cooking 5–6 pieces at a time and turning when the **pakoras** are a golden colour. the **pakoras** should be ready after 2–3 minutes. remove with a slotted spoon and drain on paper towels. serve while still warm, accompanied by refreshingly tangy **raita**.

RAITA
[cucumber and yoghurt dip]

whisk together the yoghurt, mint, lemon juice, ginger and garlic. mix in the shredded cucumber, salt to taste and, if desired, stir in honey.

heat the oil in small saucepan and fry the seeds until they pop. add the seeds to the yoghurt and mix well. chill and serve as an accompaniment to almost any spicy dish.

Serves 4–6

BATTER
2 tsp ghee
1 tsp baking soda
1 1/2 cups besan
(see glossary)
1 tsp garam masala
1 tsp ground coriander
1 tsp chilli powder
1/2 tsp ground turmeric
salt, to taste
1/2 cup water

FILLING
3 large onions, finely
sliced
2.5cm (1in) piece ginger,
grated
1/2 cup chopped coriander
leaves
vegetable oil,
for deep-frying

Makes about 3 cups

1 1/2 cups full-cream
yoghurt
1/2 cup chopped mint
juice of 1 lemon
2.5cm (1in) piece ginger,
grated
1 clove garlic, crushed
1 large cucumber, peeled,
seeded and shredded
salt
1 tbsp honey (optional)
2 tbsp vegetable oil
1 tsp cumin seeds or
black mustard seeds

1/2 cup red lentils, picked
over and rinsed
2 cups water
2 tbsp ghee
1 tsp brown mustard
seeds
1 tsp cumin seeds
2 tsp asafoetida
(see glossary)
1 onion, finely sliced
1 potato, cut into 2cm
(3/4in) cubes
3 tomatoes, cut into
quarters
1 cup tamarind water
(see glossary)
salt and freshly ground
black pepper
2 tsp sambar powder
(see glossary)
2 dried red chillies
2 dried curry leaves
(see glossary)
1 cup water

SAMBAR
[vegetables in tamarind broth]

Sambar *has many different incarnations — it ranges from a watery
consistency with fire in abundance to a thick vegetable gravy or stew,
tempered with yoghurt or buttermilk. Served traditionally with* tiffin
(for example, **dosa**, **vadai** *or* **idli***), they can also find their way onto a*
thali *tray or be eaten with nothing more than plain rice.*

place the lentils and water in a heavy-based saucepan. bring to the boil, reduce heat and simmer until almost the consistency of puree, about 1 1/2–2 hours. set aside.

heat the ghee in another large, heavy-based saucepan and gently fry the mustard seeds, cumin seeds and *asafoetida* until the mustard seeds pop. add the onion, potato and tomatoes and stir until well coated. add the tamarind water, salt and pepper to taste, *sambar* powder, dried chillies and curry leaves. add more water to cover, if necessary. reduce heat, add the cooked lentils and simmer until the vegetables are very soft, about 30 minutes. remove from heat and serve.

[
note: green beans, capsicums, eggplant and okra all make tasty additions to this soup.
]

IDLI
[steamed rice dumplings]

Serves 6–8

1 *cup* urad dhal *(husked black lentils), rinsed and soaked overnight in* 2 *cups water*
2 *cups parboiled rice, soaked overnight in* 6 *cups water*
1 *cup water*
salt

These light, dry snacks are usually eaten for breakfast. Like plain rice, **idli** *absorbs the flavours of various accompaniments. I found it fascinating that, no matter where I was in southern India, the older men almost uniformly preferred* **idli** *to* **dosa** *and* **vadai**. *I don't know if these gentle dumplings are kinder to their teeth or whether through the years they have learnt the* **idli** *provided the perfect sponge to the spicy chutneys and* **sambar** *with which it is always served.*

drain the *urad dhal* and blend in a food processor or blender, adding water as necessary to make a thick paste. repeat this process with the rice. combine the blended *dhal* and rice in a bowl and add salt to taste. set aside overnight.

Just prior to cooking, it is vital to beat the batter — the incorporation of air will ensure a lighter result. shape the batter into balls the size of golf balls, flatten slightly, and arrange in a steaming basket. steam until firm and rubbery, about 15 minutes. alternatively, place the balls in a muffin tray submerged in water and steam as above.

serve hot with **sambar** (see recipe opposite) and chutney, although they are delicious eaten cold, too.

THAIR VADAI
[crispy lentil dumplings in coconut yoghurt]

VADAI MIXTURE
1 cup urad dhal (husked black lentils), rinsed and soaked overnight in
2 cups water
2 green chillies, chopped
1 tsp black peppercorns
1 tsp cumin seeds
salt, to taste
1 tsp asafoetida (see glossary)
1/2 cup coriander leaves

vegetable oil, for deep-frying

COCONUT YOGHURT
1 tbsp ghee
1 tsp brown mustard seeds
2 cups yoghurt
1/2 cup freshly grated coconut or shredded coconut
salt

GARNISH
2 birdseye chillies, sliced
1 tbsp coriander leaves

The night had glided by on the bow of the ageing ferry that plows the backwaters between Cochin and Ernakulam. The stars were out in force and the water was liquid glass, broken only by lilies and the shimmering lanterns of shrimp fisher-folk. We sat in silence, admiring the palm trees silhoutted in the full moon and listening to the meditational lull of the putt-putt engine. By daybreak we were in Cochin, delivered into the clutches of a market in full swing. Ravenous, we found a tiffin vendor whose customers were clamouring for a sample of his wares. Although vadai are usually served plain with condiments, this particular recipe comes from an attempt to replicate the version which soothed our hunger that morning.

VADAI: drain the *urad dhal*, place in a food processor or blender with a little water and blend to a smooth paste. add the remaining **vadai** ingredients and a little extra water to facilitate blending — the paste should be just firm enough to mould. shape the paste into golf ball-sized balls with your hands — the mixture should yield about 10–12 balls. flatten each ball slightly and then make a hole in the centre so it resembles a small doughnut.

heat the oil to very hot and lower the **vadai** balls gently into the oil — they should float to the surface and expand slightly. (it will probably be necessary to do this in batches.) cook until golden and crisp, about 3 minutes each side. remove and drain.

COCONUT YOGHURT: heat the ghee in a heavy-based frying pan and fry the mustard seeds until they pop. in a mixing bowl, whisk together the mustard seeds, yoghurt and coconut until creamy, and add salt to taste.

to serve, place the **vadai** into the yoghurt mixture and sprinkle over the garnish — and watch those chillies!

CHAI
[indian tea]

In Mysore the spice market looks for all the world like a surrealist's
palate. So too the food — it mirrors the colours with its complex
flavours and captivating aromas. Walking around the assorted stalls,
piled high with dried chillies, fruits, sandlewood (Mysore is known
as the sandlewood carving capital of India), and conical mounds of
ground spice and fluorescent dye, I came to rest at a **chai** *stop.*

Chai *in India is not simply tea. It is a pastime and a skill that if not*
carried out to perfection, results in a very short career.
The fresh milk of a Brahmin cow is combined with tea leaves,
a stick of cinnamon, a few cardamom pods, freshly sliced ginger,
a clove or two, some fresh nutmeg, ground coriander and a couple of
kilograms of sugar. In fact, every **chai** *wallah has a 'secret' recipe,*
and some even combine spices normally reserved for curries,
garam masala being a popular choice. The **chai** *is then brought to the*
boil a number of times and poured into two 'cooling' jugs.
The vendor then 'stretches' the **chai** *by pouring one jug into another*
and widening the distance between the jugs as he goes. This is done in
such quick succession back and forth that the **chai** *appears like a*
thick, milky, elastic band. Glasses are then filled and promptly
offered. The whole point is not so much to mix the blend but to cool
the **chai** *and aerate the milk so it can be consumed immediately.*
Still, my addiction to this morning crusade and the pace with which
I emptied my glass earnt me the nickname 'iron throat'
from my more genteel, sipping partner.

THALI
[mixed plate]

Thali *is a one-person buffet that always includes rice,* **dhal,** *bread (either* puri,

paratha *or* chapati)**, sambar,** *a vegetable curry or stew* (sabzi)*, fresh yoghurt,*

pickles and, according to the day, a 'special'. They are almost universally served

on a metal platter with several compartments or — in the case of roadside stalls

or on the beach — on nothing more than a freshly washed banana leaf.

So while they may be best described as a banquet, they in fact make up the main

meal of the day for both rich and poor. And of course they are bottomless — the

vendor will come around and keep dishing up until you signal you've had enough.

To prepare your own **thali,** *I suggest some plain white rice,* **channa dhal,**

sambar, keralan prawns *and, for vegetarians,* **palak paneer**

(or use the filling for the **aloo mattar samousas)**, **raita** *and poppadums.*

And don't forget the addition of **aam achar.**

Makes about 2 cups

6 medium unripe
mangoes
1 tbsp salt, or to taste
$^1/_2$ cup sesame oil
1 tbsp coriander seeds
1 tsp fenugreek seeds
1 tbsp brown mustard
seeds
2 tbsp vinegar
1 tbsp palm sugar or
brown sugar
1 tbsp chilli powder
1 tbsp asafoetida
(see glossary)

AAM ACHAR
[mango pickle]

cut each mango lengthwise, remove the seed, slice into sixteen segments and rub in the salt. heat a little of the oil and fry the coriander seeds until fragrant. grind the seeds in a mortar and return to the pan. add the remaining oil, fenugreek seeds and mustard seeds and fry until the seeds pop. remove from heat, stir in the vinegar, sugar, chilli powder and *asafoetida,* and allow to cool completely.

place the mango in an airtight jar, pour in spiced oil to cover, and seal. every second day, turn the jar on its end to make sure every piece of mango is pickling. after 2 weeks the pickle will be ready and, provided the mango is covered with the spiced oil, it will keep for up to 6 months. serve as an accompaniment to almost any indian dish.

KERALAN PRAWNS

Under a tightly knit canopy of coconut palms where the heat couldn't penetrate, I found respite. Sinewy locals worked the cantilevered fishing nets — like giant shadow puppets against an impossible azure sea, they were swung, lowered and lifted, and the tiniest catch returned to the shore. The produce was then brought up the beach to the cooks' huts and turned instantly into a gourmet meal. With all the ingredients laid out before them, the cooks went to work concocting simple, tasty dishes to order in minutes.

2 tbsp vegetable oil
2 onions, finely sliced
2 cloves garlic, chopped
5cm (2in) piece ginger, grated
2 tbsp freshly grated coconut mixed with 2 tbsp water, or ¹/₂ cup coconut cream
2 birdseye chillies, chopped
1 tsp ground coriander
1 tsp ground turmeric
1 tsp ground cumin
500g (1lb) uncooked prawns, peeled and deveined
squeeze of lemon
¹/₂ cup chopped coriander leaves

heat the oil in a wok and fry the onions on high heat until translucent, about 1–2 minutes. add the garlic, ginger, coconut, chillies, coriander, turmeric and cumin and fry until fragrant, about 1 minute. add the prawns and stir-fry until they turn bright pink, about 3–4 minutes. squeeze over lemon juice, add the coriander leaves, toss and serve.

250g (8oz) minced pork
1 cup finely chopped
chinese cabbage
$^{1}/_{2}$ cup chopped spring
onions (scallions)
1 tbsp rice wine vinegar
1 tbsp soy sauce
1 tsp grated ginger
1 tsp sesame oil
salt and freshly ground
black pepper
1 packet round dim sim
or wonton wrappers
1 tbsp cornflour mixed
with a little water
vegetable oil, for frying

MOMOS
[fried dumplings]

'Freak Street' is, as its name suggests, a place for the congregation
of the bizarre. Coined during Kathmandu's heyday as the mecca for
blissed-out travellers and hallucinogenic trail riders, it now seems a
little tired from the continual attention of the western tourist. Much of
the traditional cuisine has made room for the demands of tourists,
however there are still plenty of places that cater for the meagre needs
of the locals. One such place, right down the end of 'Freak Street', is
a little Tibetan hideaway where they serve nothing more than a
handful of variations of the **momo**. The closest approximation I can
think of is Chinese gyoza, although this does no justice to the
uniqueness and juiciness of **momos.**

in a large mixing bowl, combine the pork, cabbage, spring onions, vinegar, soy sauce, ginger, sesame oil and salt and pepper to taste. mix well and set aside for 30 minutes.

place 1 tablespoon of the pork mixture in the centre of each dim sim wrapper. brush the edges with a little of the cornflour mixture and pinch the edges together to form a crescent-shaped dumpling.

in a heavy-based frying pan, heat enough oil to cover the bottom by about 5mm ($^{1}/_{4}$in). add as many of the **momos** as will fit snugly, with the pinched edges facing up. fry on low heat for a few minutes until the bottom is nicely browned, then pour in $^{1}/_{4}$ cup water and immediately cover tightly. let the **momos** steam until the water has evaporated, about 4–5 minutes. lift the **momos** out gently and serve immediately.

TIBETAN BREAD

Makes 10

2 cups atta *(see glossary)*
or 1^1/$_2$ cups wholemeal
flour mixed with ^{1}/$_2$ cup
plain flour
^{1}/$_2$ tsp salt
2 tbsp ghee, softened,
plus extra
^{1}/$_2$ cup warm water
vegetable oil,
for deep-frying

At 4400 metres, and a day ahead of me that included a 900-metre climb followed by a 1500-metre descent, a hearty breakfast was needed. It would be a sound idea, I thought, to follow the eating habits of the hardy locals. The yak butter tea I had tried before and not found at all appetising. But the fried bread, drizzled with honey, that was a treat! — and not unlike a rustic version of the French toast the Nikon-wielding warriors were devouring back in Kathmandu.

sift the flour into a bowl, sprinkle over the salt and rub the ghee into the flour with your fingertips, until the mixture is the consistency of breadcrumbs. pour in warm water and work quickly to incorporate it into the flour. add a little of the remaining water at a time until a kneadable dough is formed. transfer the dough to a floured surface and continue kneading for at least 10–15 minutes. roll the dough into a ball, rub with ghee and allow to rest for 30–60 minutes.

knead the dough for a further 3–4 minutes and roll into a log about 20cm (8in) long. cut into 10 equal portions and roll each portion into a ball. using a rolling pin, flatten each ball into a circle approximately 20cm (8in) in diameter. make 3 incisions in each circle, one in the centre and one on either side, cutting all the way through but taking care not to get too close to the edge.

heat the oil in a deep pan or wok and, when very hot, gently slip in one circle of bread. it should rise to the surface after a few seconds so, using the back of a slotted spoon, keep it submerged until it puffs up, about 30–60 seconds. carefully turn the bread over and fry the other side until golden brown. drain on paper towels and serve immediately.

Serves 6–8

2 tbsp ghee
1 tbsp black mustard
seeds
3 onions, finely chopped
5cm (2in) piece ginger,
grated
3 cloves garlic, crushed
1 tsp ground turmeric
4 red chillies, seeded and
finely chopped
6 medium potatoes,
cooked and mashed
1 cup chopped coriander
salt and freshly ground
black pepper

BATTER
3 cups besan
(see glossary)
3 tsp asafoetida
(see glossary)
salt, to taste
$1/2$ cup vegetable oil
water
vegetable oil,
for deep-frying

ALOO BONDA
[spiced potato balls]

Popular throughout India, I also ate these from a wallah *who did*
a brisk trade below the temple of the Kamari.

heat the ghee in a frying pan and stir-fry the mustard seeds until they begin to pop. add the onions, ginger and garlic and cook, stirring, for a few minutes, then add the turmeric and chillies and cook for a few minutes more. transfer to a mixing bowl with the mashed potato and chopped coriander. season with salt and pepper, mix well, roll into golf ball-sized balls and set aside.

to make the batter, combine the *besan, asafoetida* and salt in a bowl. add the oil and just enough water to make a thick batter of pouring consistency.

heat the oil in a heavy-based saucepan until smoking. dip the potato balls in the batter, shake off any excess and gently place them in the hot oil. deep-fry until golden, drain on paper towels and serve with chutney (such as **aam achar** on page 78) or **raita** (page 73).

DHAL
[spinach puree]

Serves 4

Kathmandu has two sister cities, Patan and Bhaktapur,

both of which at one time or another were the capitals of

the Nepalese empire. While Darmar Square in Patan is astonishingly

beautiful, it was the Mahbouda Temple, with its thousand or so

tranquil buddhas, that I found remarkable.

Crammed into mud-bricked suburbia, it provides a fascinating insight

into how much religion is woven into the everyday.

Just outside there was a young girl dishing out spinach **dhal** *on tin*

plates that could have served as the breast armour for the charge of

the Light Brigade they were so battered. I managed to eat half of it

before the chilli hit. I smiled valiantly — a vain attempt to

maintain an embarrassed composure while beads of sweat betrayed

my western tongue. Tears streaming down my face,

I ran to the nearest shop where the proprietor made a small fortune

selling me bottled water. This recipe is somewhat tamer.

1 tbsp ghee
1 tsp black mustard seeds
1 tsp cumin seeds
1 tsp asafoetida
(see glossary)
2 tsp black peppercorns
1 tsp coriander seeds
1 red chilli, chopped
1/2 cup red lentils, picked
over and rinsed
1 cup chopped spinach
1 cup tamarind water
(see glossary)
1 tsp grated ginger
2 cups water
salt and freshly ground
black pepper

heat the ghee in a heavy-based frying pan and fry the mustard seeds, cumin seeds, *asafoetida*, peppercorns, coriander seeds and chilli until fragrant, about 2–3 minutes. add the lentils and continue stirring for 3 minutes. remove from heat and blend in a food processor or blender. return the paste to the frying pan and stir in the spinach, tamarind water, ginger and water. season to taste with salt and pepper and simmer for 10 minutes.

serve over plain white rice, with **aloo bonda** (see recipe opposite) and **raita** (page 73) on the side.

egypt

Very few countries fire the western imagination as Egypt does. Fascinating in its heritage and famed as the cradle of modern civilisation, Egypt has borne witness to many of the conflicts that have shaped the region into its present form and, consequently, the rest of Europe.

The pockmarks of those battles are heavily embossed into the country's fabric and can be seen and felt in the everyday – from the stub-like nose of the Sphinx (used by Turkish soldiers as target practise) to the proud and resilient psyche of the people. The Egyptian people wear their country's past with spirited enthusiasm, yet the legacy is to continually strive for the internal recognition, acceptance and importance they once had.

While reference to Egypt's history cannot be made without paying homage to the architectural majesty of the Pharoahs, the street food that has survived is very much 'of the people'. Although not a complex cuisine, it has evolved by combining the many and varied influences of countless crusades and incursions: the nuts, dates pulses and spices that tie the Egyptian kitchen irrevocably to its Arabic brothers; the use of pita, kebabs and felafel that has connections throughout the Middle East; and the yoghurt, 'pizza' and cooking techniques whisper of the

southern European influence. It is also a cuisine of regionality – notably the seafood or Alexandria and the Red Sea coast, and the reliance on beans and salted or dried goods reflects the semi-nomadic, desert existence.

Although Egypt is not blessed with the ability to produce a variety of foods itself, it is geographically a centre for trade and exchange: to the north and northwest there are the Greek isles, the Peloponnese and Italy; to the northeast there is Israel, Palestine and Lebanon; to the west one moves along the coast of North Africa; to the south along the Nile River there is greater Africa; and to the southeast the Indian Ocean and the Far East. If the idea to build a mansion anywhere in the world appeals, Egypt boasts 360-degree views.

When it comes to agriculture there's one vital ingredient that sums up both Egypt's potential and its limitations – the Nile. It has always been the regulator of the Egyptian agricultural calendar and traditionally splits the year into three seasons: flood, recovery and 'the dry'. Perhaps no other country in the world is so dependent upon a single course of water as is Egypt.

Aswan is the last major settlement on the banks of the Egyptian Nile, a market town for the Nubian traders since time immemorial. It is also the gateway to the Sudan and greater Africa. Here goods from as far as the Mediterranean arrived, passed from *felucca* to *felucca* (the traditional sailing boats) and traded for jewellery, precious stones, artefacts and dried goods. These days the town has assumed a certain majesty, with riverside cafes, hotels and boulevards, and rows of gently rocking *feluccas*. I can think of no better place to enjoy a sunset chrysanthemum tea. Here street food still thrives, especially at the market where the local version of mujadarra still bespeaks the diet of the nomadic desert traders.

South from Aswan, a pre-dawn trip in a desert-weathered Peugeot delivered us to a monument in megalomania – Abu Simbel. A massive temple complex built by Ramases 11, to align his image alongside that of the gods, greets the blood orange sunrise with equal parts arrogance and respect. The trip itself is a life experience, where drivers rally each other along a pot-holed highway that occasionally disappears under the shifting desert sands.

A cruise along the Nile on a *felucca* provides an insight into the daily rituals of those dependent on the river for their livelihood. Gliding within inches of the shoreline, we traded smile with farmers tilling the soil with flimsy hoes, groups of chatter-happy women beating their washing upon an overturned boat and grubby-cheeked children racing down to meet their papa. On one such occasion at Edfu, we were taken ashore and introduced to the captain's wife, who proudly offered us some freshly baked **aish** (Egyptian pita) as we squatted on the dirt kitchen floor. Our *felucca* drifted past crumbling temples, propelled by the current in the morning and a stiffening breeze in the afternoon. We watched cloudless skies give way to star-drenched evenings and swatted mosquitoes into the dead still of the night. This was the magic of Egypt at work, and while our eyes feasted, our appetites were sustained by simplicity itself – **fulmedames**, rice, **aish** and **chopped salad**. When we disembarked at Luxor, it was with sadness and excitement, for ahead lay the valley of the Kings and a journey of a different sort, into ancient Egypt.

Cairo is a city of pulse and frantic energy. At first impression one could be forgiven for believing that the city is run on panic

– so high is the level of confusion and so insistent are the people – one can feel overwhelmed by the assault on the senses. However, it is also a city of sombre reflection and devout power, especially in the maze of buckled cobblestone streets that is referred to as 'Old Cairo'. Before the first rays of daybreak, the city of Islam musters the faithful to mosques which are as old as the religion itself. Within a few hours, the serpentine alleys transform into a writhing market, humming with vitality. Here it is possible to buy anything and meet face-to-face with the generosity and acute business sense of the Egyptian trader. You can sense the challenge – the less likely one is to buy, the more effort the vendor applies to their craft. Old men crouched under the clouds of blue smoke that waft from their ever-glowing hookah pipes, beckon you into the backroom of their carpet shop, while tinsmiths, papyrus artists and the incessant tug of the beggars vie for the chance that you may cross their palms with silver.

Suddenly the arts and crafts give way to food. Nuts, dried fruit, fresh vegetables and herbs abound in quantity if not variety, while the spice section would drive an aromatherapist into a shopping frenzy.

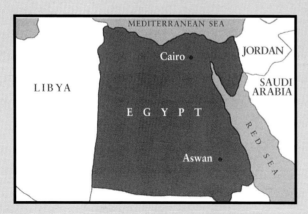

In the homes and on the streets of the smaller provincial towns, life moves at a much slower pace. An old custom that survives, especially in smaller provincial towns, is the way bakeries are still revered as the community kitchen – a good place to base one's forays into the local cuisine. And what could be more alluring than waiting and watching as your bread and pastry is kneaded and then baked right in front of you by the warmth of their ovens? Sipping on tea from the well-placed café next door, watching a parade of women bringing in their stews or breads to be slow cooked in the wood-fired ovens and falling prey to the intoxicating aroma that carves ceremony into the atmosphere.

The sights, sounds and smells of Egypt are mesmerising. It is common to see even well-seasoned travellers stumbling around Cairo completely dazed – heady with an overdose of perfume samples, their senses rattled by the perpetual crush, surrounded by the starched uniforms of the *Mongumma* (tourist police), and being wolf-whistled by the young soldiers sporting maniacal grins and machine guns slung carelessly over their shoulders. All this seems a world away from the serenity of a camel trek on the Red Sea coast, witnessing the sunrise from atop Mount Sinai or exploring the icy tombs of the Valley of the Kings. Wherever one turns, Egypt never fails to fill the traveller with a sense of timeless ambience.

Perhaps nowhere in the Arab world is the ongoing struggle between tradition and the encroaching march of modernisation so fiercely fought as it is in Egypt, for while it is geographically part of Africa, Egypt is essentially an Arabic culture; a country that exists at the crossroads of civilisations, both past and present.

FUL MEDAMES
[egyptian beans]

Serves 6–8

1kg (2lb) Egyptian brown beans (ful), *soaked overnight in water to cover (see note)*

GARLIC AND LEMON PASTE
4 cloves garlic, chopped
1/4 cup olive oil
juice of 2 lemons
2 tsp ground cumin
salt and freshly ground black pepper
2 lemons, cut into wedges

SALAD
1 large red onion, thinly sliced
1 clove garlic, chopped
1 large tomato, chopped
a few sprigs of coriander, chopped (optional)
a little olive oil

You can't go to Egypt and not taste **ful medames.** *You simply cannot! A dish that supposedly even the Pharaohs would summon, it is now no less than the undisputed national dish and a mirror of Egyptian society itself: simple, earthy and wholesome. It can be found on every street corner from Alexandria to Aswan, its aroma swimming with the first rays of the sun.* **Ful medames** *are served in small white bowls with a wedge of lemon. When you've finished eating, the bowl is returned to a bucket of water, wiped and then promptly refilled for the next customer — when eating from street-side vendors, you quickly adapt to the ways ... or starve!*

cook the beans gently over low heat for 2 hours or until very soft, but not mushy (although the first thing many egyptians do is mash their beans, it is usually left up to the diner). by the time the beans are done they will have absorbed all the cooking liquid and released enough starch and colour to form a thick sauce.

to make the paste, mix together the garlic, olive oil, lemon juice and cumin, and season to taste with salt and pepper. serve in a separate dish to the beans.

to make the salad, combine all the salad ingredients in a bowl and moisten with a little olive oil.

to serve, place a ladleful of *ful* in each of 6–8 small bowls, top with a teaspoon of chopped salad, half a **hamine egg** (page 88) and a wedge of lemon. pass around the garlic and lemon paste.

[**note**: *ful* are available from middle eastern food stores, but if you are unable to find them, use brown lentils instead.]

BEID HAMINE
[hamine eggs]

Breakfast in Cairo can be as simple as a couple of **beid hamine,** *some*
aish (pita bread) and a spoonful of chopped salad (see **ful medames***).*
There are vendors who sell nothing but eggs and little sachets of salt mixed
with cumin — surprisingly, some vendors are far more successful than others.
The woman who swept the egg-shell remnants from my hotel floor explained why:
the secret is patience. Traditionally, a large clay pot is left on the exhausted
coals overnight, the eggs barely simmering in a stock of whatever's left over
from dinner — onion skins and garlic being the only true requisites.
The following morning the eggs are ready. The prolonged cooking renders the yolk
an extra-creamy texture while the stock permeates the shell. Sometimes the eggs
are simply cooked along with whatever stew is 'on the go'.

The difference is worth the effort.

Serves 4

4 large onions, peeled
2 tbsp olive oil
1 cup brown lentils,
soaked for a few hours
in water to cover, then
drained
2 cloves garlic, crushed
1 tsp ground cumin
1 tsp ground coriander
1 cup long-grain rice
salt and freshly ground
black pepper
1 lemon, cut into wedges

MUJADARRA
[lentils and rice]

Peasant food. No ifs, no buts. Yet it's a dish that, like **ful medames,**
shines with simple integrity. On the smallest of street corners,
vendors spoon out **mujadarra** *to the poor and the rich,*
for it is a dish of union that will appease any hunger.

finely dice 2 onions. heat half the olive oil in a large saucepan and fry the diced onions on low until browned. add the drained lentils, garlic, ground spices and enough water to cover and cook on low until the lentils are still a little firm, about 20 minutes.

add the rice and enough water to cover, season with salt and pepper and continue to simmer until the rice is done, about 15 minutes — watch carefully in case more water is needed.

slice the remaining 2 onions into thick rings and fry very gently in remaining olive oil until almost caramelised. serve the lentils and rice on a large platter, top with the onion rings and a little oil, and surround with lemon wedges.

KOFTA MLEBISSA
[kofta in batter]

Sunrise on Mount Sinai ... as the desert shadows surrendered to the
brutality of an Egyptian sun, I began the descent down the
thousand-odd steps a single monk had built as penance. I'm not sure if
it was fear of the same fate, the heat or the thought of following in
the footsteps of Moses that had me blessing the vendor at the base
— a purveyor of the finest **kofta.**

Serves 4

1/2 cup basmati rice
500g (1lb) minced beef
2 onions, chopped
2 cloves garlic, crushed
11/2 cups chopped parsley
11/2 cups chopped mint
2 tsp ground cinnamon
salt and freshly ground
black pepper
1 cup water
2 eggs, beaten
1/2 cup plain flour
1 tsp baking powder
1/2 cup warm water
vegetable oil,
for deep-frying

wash the rice and mix well with the minced beef, onions, garlic, parsley, mint and spices. season to taste with salt and pepper. with wet hands, mould the mixture into walnut-sized balls and set aside.

bring 1 cup water to the boil in a wide-based saucepan. carefully place in the koftas and cook over low heat until done, about 12–15 minutes. remove gently and set aside to cool.

mix the eggs with the flour and baking powder, adding warm water as necessary to form a thick batter. heat enough oil for deep-frying, dip the koftas in batter and place them in the hot oil. cook until golden, about 2–3 minutes, and drain on paper towels.

serve with **salsa.**

SALSA

Makes about 2 cups

500g (1lb) tomatoes,
peeled (see note) and
chopped
4 cloves garlic, crushed
2 tbsp chopped parsley
2 red chillies, seeded and
finely chopped
1 cinnamon stick
1 tbsp ground cumin
2 tbsp brown sugar
salt and freshly ground
black pepper, to taste
juice of 2 lemons

in a heavy-based saucepan, bring all the ingredients, except the lemon juice, to the boil. simmer for 40 minutes, check for seasoning, allow to cool and stir in the lemon juice.

[**note:** to peel tomatoes, cut a cross in the bottom and blanch in boiling water for 30 seconds. drop into cold water and peel off the skin with your fingers.]

TA'AMIA

[felafels]

1 cup chickpeas, soaked
overnight in water to
cover
1 cup broad beans,
soaked overnight in water
to cover
1/2 cup diced onion
4 cloves garlic, crushed
1/2 cup sesame seeds
1/2 cup besan
(see glossary)
1/4 cup fine burghul
(see glossary)
2 tsp ground cumin
2 tsp ground coriander
2 tsp baking powder
1 tsp cayenne
1/2 cup chopped parsley
1/2 tbsp salt
1 cup water
(approximately)
vegetable oil,
for deep-frying

The actual birthplace of many Middle Eastern dishes is hidden
amongst claims and counterclaims, just as the territory is, though
that's not to say that each culture is not defiantly distinct! In the case
of the humble **felafel**, *there are almost a dozen varieties.*
This particular interpretation differs from the classic Lebanese
and Israeli versions in the combination of ingredients —
which, for me, make a superior **felafel**.

drain the chickpeas and beans and blend in a food processor or blender until a coarse paste is formed. transfer to a large bowl and mix in the remaining ingredients, except the oil, adding just enough water to hold the mixture together. set aside for up to 3 hours.

using your hands or two spoons, mould the **felafel** mixture into walnut-sized patties. (in egypt, the mixture is packed into traditional **felafel** moulds.) heat the oil in a heavy-based saucepan and deep-fry the **felafels** until crunchy and golden. drain on paper towels. serve with **aish** (page 93), **tarator bi tahina** (page 95) and/or yoghurt, a few slices of tomato and shredded lettuce.

OPPOSITE: indian thali, consisting of **channa dhal** — chickpea dip [page 69], **paratha** — flaky bread [page 70], **palak paneer** — spiced spinach puree [page 72], and **raita** — cucumber and yoghurt dip [page 73]

AISH
[pita bread]

Aish is to Egypt what rice is to Asia — no meal would be complete without it. The earthiness of fresh wholemeal pita is such that it's good enough to eat on its own. Although replaced for the most part by bleached flour for its softness and pliability, I prefer the homeliness of wholemeal.

dissolve the yeast in the warm water and set aside for 15–20 minutes. sift the flours and salt into a large bowl and mix in the yeast. to make a 'richer' dough, incorporate the butter. knead the dough for 10 minutes, cover with a damp cloth and leave in a warm place to rise for about 3 hours.

knead the dough for a further 3 minutes then roll into a log, about 5cm (2in) in diameter, and cut into 12 equal pieces. egyptian pita is often pulled into a tear-drop shape, which makes for a lighter bread, but a rolling pin works almost as well. roll each piece into an oval shape and place on an ungreased baking tray in a moderate oven (180°C/350°F). bake for 10–12 minutes and serve hot.

Makes 12

4 tsp dry yeast
2 cups warm water
3 cups wholemeal flour
3 cups plain white flour
2 tsp salt
2 tbsp butter (optional)

FATOUSH
[pita salad]

This is an unusual salad — toasted aish is treated like a vegetable and tossed with the dressing. I always found it intriguing the way Egyptians would tear up their aish and toss it amongst the salad, to be scooped up with their fingers along with the tart lemon and garlic dressing.

whisk together the dressing ingredients and set aside.

combine all the salad ingredients, pour over half the dressing and toss well. traditionally the salad is left to absorb the flavours for an hour before being served with the extra dressing.

OPPOSITE: **egyptian mixed plate**, consisting of **ta'amia** — felafels [page 90], **aish** — pita bread [above], **mujadarra** — lentils and rice [page 88], and chopped salad [page 87]

Serves 4

DRESSING
2 cloves garlic, chopped
1/2 cup lemon juice
1/2 cup olive oil
salt and freshly ground
black pepper, to taste

SALAD
3 medium tomatoes, cut
into small chunks
1 telegraph cucumber, cut
into small chunks
1 cos lettuce, shredded
1/2 cup chopped parsley
1/4 cup chopped mint
1 green pepper, diced
1 aish, toasted and cut
into squares

MURABYAN
[red sea prawns]

1kg (2lb) fresh uncooked
prawns (preferably tiger
prawns)
2 tbsp sea salt
$1/2$ cup plain flour
4 tbsp butter
4 tbsp olive oil
2 onions, chopped
4 cloves garlic, chopped
1 tbsp paprika
$1/2$ cup chopped
coriander leaves
juice of 2 limes

*Sharm El Sheikh and Dahab are popular tourist haunts despite the
harsh nature of what lies inland — the Sinai Desert. The Sinai
Peninsula, handed back to the Egyptians in 1972 after the 1968
war with Israel, is a remarkable blend of Arab and Bedouin culture,
but the sight of burnt-out wrecks, like pages torn from the book of
history, litter the highways and keep the memory of occupation close
to the surface. In contrast to this, there are beaches of utter beauty,
set against the stark desolation of desert mountains and fringed with
coral rich in tropical sea life. Where there are tourists, cafes abound
like extended beach parties. This dish is simple and popular with the
hordes descending from the dry interior.*

leaving the last segment and tail intact, clean, shell and devein the prawns. toss them in sea salt, dust with flour and shake off any excess.

heat the butter and oil in a heavy-based frying pan and sauté the onions until transparent. add the garlic, paprika and prawns, tossing constantly. when the prawns are golden, add the coriander, toss and remove from heat. stir in the lime juice and serve immediately.

SAMAK MAQULI
[fried fish]

Serves 4

1kg (2lb) whole fresh fish
(such as red mullet or
sardines), cleaned and
scaled
8 cloves garlic, crushed
salt and freshly ground
black pepper
2 cups chopped parsley
1 cup plain flour
olive oil, for deep-frying
lemon wedges

It can be on a dust-hazy main street of Cairo, during the crazed
haggling of a street bazaar, or in the solitude of a lone hawker on a
beach at sunset when it nabs you — the aroma of fried fish.
Telltale parcels of oil-slicked newspaper mark the way to a hawker
well-practised in the simple yet sacred art of frying fish.

rub the fish with garlic, salt and pepper and stuff with the remaining garlic and the parsley. dust with flour and set aside.

heat the oil in a heavy-based saucepan until it begins to smoke. (it is vital when frying fish to keep the temperature high, otherwise the fish will become saturated in oil rather than sealed by it). deep-fry a few fish at at time, according to the size of the pan. cook until crisp and golden — about 3–5 minutes, depending on the size of the fish — and drain immediately on paper towels. serve hot with a wedge of lemon and **tarator bi tahina** (below).

TARATOR BI TAHINA
[tahini sauce]

Makes about 2 cups

1 cup tahini
(see glossary)
4 cloves garlic, crushed
1/4 cup lemon juice
1/2 cup water
1 tbsp chopped parsley
salt and freshly ground
black pepper

There is a rich man's and a poor man's sauce for fish. In the
restaurants that line the tourist burrows, they blend bucketloads of
semi-precious pine nuts with bread, garlic, lemon juice and fish stock.
The result is sublime. On the street, however, such refinery is not
even noticed as the locals lick from their fingers this easy,
nourishing and classic combination.

in a mixing bowl, beat the tahini with the garlic and lemon juice, adding the water a little at a time until a smooth, pouring consistency is attained. mix in the parsley and season with salt and pepper to taste.

SAYYADIEH

[fish with rice]

4 tbsp olive oil
4 onions, thinly sliced
4 cups water
1 tsp salt
2 tsp ground cumin
2 sprigs thyme
1kg (2lb) cod or bream fillets
500g (1lb) basmati rice
juice of 1 lemon
50g (2oz) pine nuts, lightly fried, to garnish

I don't know of a better combination than well-poached fish served with rice cooked in the stock. One of the most memorable examples I've ever eaten was prepared and served on the banks of the Nile, where feluccas jostled in the wake of the futuristic ferries on their sightseeing rounds.

heat the oil in a heavy-based frying pan and fry the onions until soft. add the water, salt, cumin and sprigs of thyme and simmer for 5 minutes. add the fish and cook gently for about 10 minutes. remove the fish to a plate and keep moist with a little of the cooking stock. reserve stock.

wash the rice, place it in a heavy-based saucepan and pour in stock to cover by 3cm (1$^1/_4$ in). bring to the boil, reduce heat and simmer until all the stock is absorbed and the rice is cooked.

spoon the rice onto a serving platter, lay the fish fillets over the top and scatter with fried pine nuts. mix the lemon juice with remaining stock, pour over the top and serve.

SHAWARMA
[marinated lamb on a skewer]

Serves 6–8

1 large leg of lamb

MARINADE
1 cup olive oil
1 tbsp salt
1 tbsp roughly ground
black peppercorns
4 onions, cut into
quarters and layers
separated
4 cloves garlic, crushed
juice of 2 lemons
1 tbsp dried rigani
(see glossary)
1 tbsp dried mint
1 tbsp ground allspice
1 tbsp ground cumin
4 large tomatoes,
finely chopped

Probably the most common of all street food in Cairo, **shawarma,**
*known as doner kebab in other Middle Eastern and some western
countries, continues to thrive. Compared with the meal-sized version
we have in western countries, the original is much smaller and far
closer to a snack; a small quantity of tender lamb that has been
well-marinated, grilled on a vertical rotisserie or spit, carved in front
of your eyes and laid in the lap of warm* **aish** *with maybe a spoonful
of yoghurt sauce (*jajik*) and lettuce. My favourite stall,
whose smoky-perfumed aroma would even induce people to attempt
crossing the street (a sure death wish in Cairo), was run by a Turkish
man who claimed eating his* **shawarma** *brought you closer to God
and improved your sex life — somewhat of a paradox I thought!*

METHOD 1: combine the marinade ingredients and rub into the leg of lamb. leave the meat to marinate for at least 6 hours, or overnight in the refrigerator. (if you do refrigerate the lamb, return it to room temperature before cooking.)

in an oven or barbecue rotisserie, cook the lamb over medium-high heat, basting with the marinade every so often and carving off slices as the outside cooks. keep the slices warm until you have enough to serve, returning to collect more as each round is finished. The whole leg will take about $1^1/_2$–2 hours to cook.

METHOD 2: combine the marinade ingredients. cut the leg of lamb into cubes, reserving any fat. thread the cubes onto skewers, interspersed with the reserved fat — this will ensure beautifully tender meat. rub the marinade into the lamb and set aside for at least 6 hours, or overnight in the refrigerator. (if you do refrigerate the lamb, return it to room temperature before cooking.)

cook the lamb skewers on a barbecue or overhead grill, turning frequently. Cook until the meat is no longer pink in the centre, about 8–10 minutes.

TO SERVE: place the lamb slices or cubes on a bed of plain white rice or on warm **aish** (page 93). serve with freshly sliced tomatoes, lettuce and a bowl of **jajik** (page 98).

3 large telegraph
cucumbers
salt
500g (1lb) thick natural
yoghurt
juice of 1 lemon
4 cloves garlic, crushed
1 tbsp olive oil
1 tbsp chopped mint
salt and freshly ground
black pepper

JAJIK
[cucumber with yoghurt sauce]

In Greece they have tzatziki. *In Turkey it's known as* tjajik. *In India, there's a variation called* **raita**. *The Lebanese, Arabs and Persians have recipes for a yoghurt-based sauce too. In some countries it is nothing more than freshly cultured sheep's or cow's milk thinned with a little lemon juice and a sprinkling of salt. But with the addition of garlic it just 'zings' on the tongue and the mint rounds out the flavour.*

grate the cucumbers and place in a colander set over a bowl. sprinkle with salt, place a weighted plate on top and leave for 1 hour to degorge. when ready, rinse and dry.

place the yoghurt, lemon juice and garlic in a mixing bowl and beat until smooth and creamy. stir in the remaining ingredients, season to taste with salt and pepper and place in the refrigerator for several hours to allow the flavours to develop before serving.

LAHMA BI AHJEEN
[arabic lamb pizza]

Disorientation as a result of excessive travelling is but one of the
joys of life on the road. Being ruled by the whims of the stomach
is another! When the two combine you can find yourself eating
the strangest things at even stranger hours of the day.
This lamb pizza is a favourite throughout Egypt, and one which
I have enjoyed many times — for breakfast!

DOUGH: dissolve the yeast in warm water and set aside for 15–20 minutes. sift the flour, sugar and salt into a large bowl and mix in the yeast. knead the dough for 15 minutes, or until very elastic. rub with a little olive oil, cover with a damp cloth and leave in warm place to rise for 3 hours.

TOPPING: in a large bowl, mix the topping ingredients with a little oil, just enough to incorporate all the spices.

TO ASSEMBLE: knead the dough for a few minutes, then shape into 8 walnut-sized balls. on a lightly floured surface, use a rolling pin to roll out each ball in a teardrop shape, about 15cm (6in) long. cover the top of each pizza base with topping, place on a greased baking tray and allow to rise for 15 minutes.

preheat the oven to very hot (230°C/450°F). bake the pizzas until lightly golden, about 7–8 minutes. serve with a sprinkling of chopped coriander and a squeeze of lemon.

DOUGH
1 tbsp fresh yeast
2 cups warm water
2 cups plain flour
pinch of sugar
pinch of salt
olive oil

TOPPING
2 onions, chopped
4 cloves garlic, crushed
4 large fresh tomatoes,
chopped
500g (1lb) minced lamb
1 tbsp tomato paste
1 tsp ground cumin
1 tsp ground allspice
1 tsp cayenne
salt, to taste
olive oil

1/2 cup chopped
coriander leaves
juice of 2 lemons

BA'AMIA

[braised okra]

2 tbsp olive oil
2 onions, chopped
2 cloves garlic, crushed
4 medium tomatoes,
chopped
500g (1lb) small okra,
soaked in vinegar for
20 minutes and drained
1 tbsp ground coriander
1 cup water
salt and freshly ground
black pepper
juice of 2 lemons
$^1/_2$ cup chopped
coriander leaves
slices of lemon

Okra, known as 'ladies' fingers' throughout much of the Middle East,
is a highly unusual vegetable and demands special treatment.
Always select baby okra that are snap-fresh and undamaged.
When they are cooked they can release a glutinous substance that is
often referred to as 'slime'. For this reason okra is almost always
cooked with tomatoes and finished with lemon, lime or vinegar.
It is quite normal for a few to burst during cooking,
but gentle simmering will prevent this happening to a certain extent.
Another way of combating this problem is to soak
the okra in vinegar before cooking. To prepare for cooking
always rinse well, cut off any hard stems without damaging the pod,
and treat gently — just like ladies' fingers!
Although most often served hot, ba'amia is sometimes served cold as
an accompaniment to grilled meats and rice. It is a versatile dish that
needs little more than some fresh bread to mop up the delectable
juices to become a light, healthy lunch, and with the addition of
chunks of lamb, it transforms into a hearty stew.

heat the olive oil in a large saucepan and fry the onions and garlic until translucent. add the tomatoes, okra, ground coriander and water and season to taste with salt and pepper. bring to the boil, then reduce heat and simmer until the okra is very soft, about 30–40 minutes. stir in the lemon juice and coriander leaves, remove from heat and allow to cool. serve with slices of lemon, warm bread and a fresh salad.

SEMIT
[sesame bread rings]

Makes about 16

*Why not make a batch of these and next time you have nothing to do
you can do what everyone in Cairo does when they've got*

nothing to do — gobble down a **semit.**
Egyptian vendors display their **semits,** *which look like giant pretzels,*

on long poles or in giant cane baskets on top of their heads.

4 tsp dry yeast
2 cups warm water
pinch of sugar
4 cups white flour
1 tbsp salt
2 tbsp butter, melted
1 egg, beaten with a
little water
1 cup sesame seeds

dissolve the yeast in $1/2$ cup of warm water, add the sugar and set aside until it begins to bubble. sift the flour and salt into a large bowl and stir in the yeast. mix in the melted butter and as much water as needed to make a stiff dough (about $1^1/2$ cups). knead the dough for 10 minutes and set aside until it has doubled in bulk, about 1 hour.

knead the dough for a few minutes, then break off walnut-sized balls and roll each ball into a rope about 1cm ($1/2$in) thick. pinch the ends together, brush with a little of the egg wash and press lightly onto a plate spread with sesame seeds. place on an oiled baking tray and set aside to rise for about 2–3 hours.

preheat the oven to 180°C (350°F). bake the **semits** for 10–12 minutes then lower the heat to 150°C (300°F) and bake for a further 15 minutes until they are golden and hollow when tapped. remove from the oven, allow to cool and store in an airtight container.

FILLING
2 cups dates, pitted and
chopped
1 cup water
2 tbsp orange water
(see glossary)
finely grated peel of half
an orange

SHORTBREAD
2 cups plain flour
1 cup butter, softened
3 tbsp rosewater
4 tbsp milk

icing sugar

MA'AMOUL
[stuffed shortbread]

*Egyptian shortbread is very fine, and instead of the overpowering
'butteryness' of the English and Scottish varieties, it has the delicate
perfume of rosewater. Egyptians also fill their shortbread with a
paste made from dates, almonds or pistachios. But no matter what the
filling,* **ma'amoul** *is a perfect accompaniment to the thick,
sweet mud Egyptians pass off as coffee.*

FILLING: place the ingredients in a heavy-based saucepan, bring to the boil, then reduce heat and simmer until the mixture reduces to a paste. be careful not to let the dates catch on the bottom. allow to cool completely.

SHORTBREAD: sift the flour into a mixing bowl and rub in the butter with your fingertips until well incorporated and the texture resembles fine breadcrumbs. add the rosewater and work it into a dough, adding the milk a little at a time until the dough holds together.

TO ASSEMBLE: pinch off walnut-sized lumps of dough, roll into balls and hollow out as if making a small pot out of clay. (the thumb is best for this at first, then carefully pinch the dough between the thumb and fingers, turning the dough in your hand to make all the sides even but not too thin). pack the hole with the date filling until three-quarters full and pinch the dough together at the top to seal. place on a floured baking tray and flatten slightly with the back of a fork.

preheat the oven to moderate (180°C/350°F) and bake the **ma'amouls** for 20 minutes. (it is very important that the shortbread remain pearly white. if they are allowed to brown, the flavour will change dramatically.) remove from oven and allow to cool on the tray, for the shortbread will be crumbly until it has fully cooled. place on a serving tray and dust with sifted icing sugar.

BASBOUSA
[semolina cake]

Serves 10–12

1/2 cup unsalted butter,
softened
1 cup caster sugar
2 eggs
2 cups fine semolina
1 tsp baking powder
1/2 tsp baking soda
1/2 cup desiccated
coconut (optional)
2 tbsp milk (optional)
blanched almonds

SYRUP
2 1/2 cups water
2 1/2 cups sugar
juice of 2 lemons
4 whole cloves
1 cinnamon stick

Just around the corner from where I stayed in Cairo, there was a little kiosk, not much larger than the wardrobe in my room, where a grumpy old woman begrudgingly sold her soul in the form of the syrup drenched, diamond-shaped cake, **basbousa.** *At first I thought it was just me — the supposedly rich foreigner — that she objected to. However, after many afternoons of close inspection, I realised she was by nature a disgruntled grouch. Maybe it was because I couldn't understand what she was saying that I actually came to like her, but one thing's for sure — it was not her customer service that caused her to sell out of* **basbousa** *by dusk every evening!*

cream the butter and sugar until light and fluffy, then add the eggs, one at a time. sift the semolina, baking powder and soda into a mixing bowl and gently fold in the butter mixture. (if you incorporate the coconut, add 2 tablespoons of milk.)

pour the batter into a greased 20cm x 30cm (8in x 12in) cake tin and score the top of the batter with diagonal lines to form diamond shapes. gently press an almond into each diamond.

preheat the oven to moderate (180°C/350°F) and bake the cake for 35–40 minutes — it should be a beautiful golden colour on top. turn out onto a cake rack.

to make the syrup, bring the water to the boil and stir in the sugar until it dissolves. add the remaining ingredients and continue to boil for a further 10 minutes. spoon the syrup all over the cake until it can absorb no more. let the cake cool and cut into diamond-shaped slices.

MOROCCO

Perched on the northwest tip of Africa, Morocco borders the Mediterranean and Atlantic Oceans, while inland gives way to the dramatic Atlas mountains and the starkness of the Sahara Desert beyond. The people of Morocco, from the lineage of the indigenous Berber tribes, down through the various marauding empires – Phoenician, Greek, Roman, Arab and French, and in combination with the influences brought back by conquests of the Moors in Spain and Portugal, have sculpted a cuisine that unites all these disparate cultures into a fusion that is uniquely their own.

It was during this period of conquest in southern Europe that the greater Moroccan empire – the moors – were the most educated, worldly and enlightened race of their time. In northern Africa, the spread of Islam created the impetus for scholars and philosophers to build upon their combined intellectual wealth with religious zeal. There were universities, known a *medersas*, created to preserve old works and translate all that was deemed worthy for the spoils of their European conquests.

It was around these schools of learning that the great cities of Morocco developed – Meknes and Fez. Food became elevated to great heights within the palaces, for it was seen as a symbol of sophistication and refinement. The by-product of this was that Moroccan street food was inundated with new methods of cooking, vessels and utensils, produce and spice. It is something, I'm glad to say, that the country continues to thrive on.

Today's Morocco, while still proud of past achievements, is humbled by its poverty. Testament to the rich diversity of the culture is everywhere, from the great *medinas* (markets) to the magnificent palaces and ornately tiled and serene mosques. Contemporary Moroccan culture is on display in the frenetic dances, the irrepressible pulse of the music and in the food that is consumed with relish every day on the streets. The country is a confusion of high-rise and horse-drawn cart, of religious tradition and secular business. While Casablanca and the capital Rabat forge themselves into cities of the future, the rest of Morocco continues at a much more 'civilised' pace, albeit with the pressure of tourism rapping on the door.

Nowhere is this confrontation more explicit than in the central square of Marrakech, Jamna El F'Na. Marrakech is unlike any other city in Morocco, for it was neither a seat of reverential learning nor is it a metropolis hell-bent on modernisation. Marrakech has always been a trading post, a market town that continues to flourish because of it is a strategic meeting place, positioned between the Berbers descending from the Atlas range, the nomadic desert traders and the merchants of the sea. The Jamna El F'Na is the chessboard where a battle of wits takes place between auctioneer, gambler and bidder; the

auditorium form where the cries of haggling ring out across the dust-smoky skies; a theatre for every kind of entertainer, magician, storyteller and shaman.

The *medinas* of Morocco are unmatched for colour and vitality, except perhaps for those in Cairo and Istanbul. The tiny, maze-like alleys resound with the tinkering and shouts of the dedicated and highly skilled craft workers who ply their proficiency with tin, leather and wood. Magnificent weavings of the infamous kilim carpets and the more intricate *djellabahs* (hooded, full-length robes) are also some of the most prized creations. To meander through the streets and witness their energy and output – for it is indeed cottage industry at its best – is to stroll back in time to a place where hand-made articles still bear the individual pride of their creator. While the average studio is little more than a few square metres, the size of the *medina* can be several square kilometres – a small

workout on the abacus suggests a *medina* is a veritable hive of workers.

To meet the demand for all this labour-intensive activity, an immense amount of food is prepared every day – as street food vendors, the Moroccans prove to be just as ingenious and the resourceful as their craft workers. The vegetable markets take over wherever there is a space, most often in small squares to enable people to wander around all that is on offer. Vendors rarely offer more than one or two varieties of produce, spread out before them on a cotton or canvas sheet. A little playful haggling is expected, with furrowed brows and machine-gun banter finally giving way to a quick exchange of goods and smiles all round.

At times the street food on offer is little more than the very produce on sale, boiled or fanned over a charcoal flame and served with a small paper cone of **spice salt**. Yet the Moroccan forte is definitely in their simmering stews and slow braises filled with fresh vegetables, often fish or chicken (meat is more expensive and subsequently less common), and heady with spice. These are known as **tagines** and are almost always served on a bed of couscous – the nation's staple.

Although bread, rice and potatoes are common companions, couscous is at the very soul of Moroccan cuisine. Along with a reliance on life-preserving quantities of garlic and ginger, there is a 'generosity' in their use of cumin, paprika and chilli, and the fresh herbs mint and coriander. Produce from the sea, particularly fish, prawns and clams (pippieds) provide much of the protein, and the Arabic influence is revealed in the combination of dried fruit and nuts in the savoury cooking process. It is a robust cuisine that has borrowed from and

redesigned the Berber, Arabic and Spanish influences to forge a style unique in seasoning and overflowing with flavours.

Beans and pulses also play an intrinsic part in the mountainous areas which do not have the fresh fish of the coastal regions. Here the African heritage shines through with the reliance on root vegetables, grains and legumes. Chickpeas are favoured as a street-side snack, soaked overnight and then fried in chilli-spiced oil, or as the main focus or a vegetarian **tagine**. Lentils and pigeon peas are used to thicken soup, while fresh green beans are delicious in a tomato, onion and olive oil braise.

Of all the stately dishes that grace the Moroccan table, perhaps none is so demanding or stunning as *b'stilla*. The literal translation is 'feathers' and indeed the many layers of filigree-like pastry are as light as the beating of a dove's wing. The traditional filling for *b'stilla* is pigeon, although chicken or *poussin* is becoming more common. The time-consuming pastry can be successfully substituted with filo, but the original filling of tender pieces of pigeon, sautéed in a little butter with almonds and delicate spices, makes it a true signature dish of the nation. Alas, a

street food it is not, and no amount of artistic licence will allow me to pass it off as such. However, many great recipes do exist for those willing to seek out the pinnacle of Moroccan cuisine.

More recently there has been an influx of western influence, most notably French. The Moroccans have refined their own pastries by taking on board some of the finesse of the French *patissier*, creating versions that are more European than those of their Arabic neighbours, yet still reminiscent of the unique blend of African and Islam.

So, the history of borrowing and re-inventing continues. In all that they touch, be it the tinsmith, leather sculptors, weavers, or artisans of the kitchen, the Moroccan people are a wonderful combination of the creative and the diligent who rejoice in the vitality of their culture.

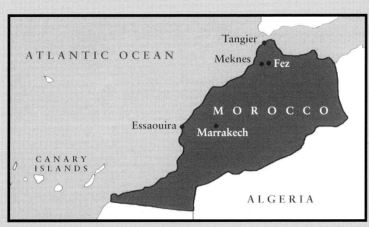

2 tbsp green tea
4 cups boiling water
4 tbsp sugar
2 bunches fresh mint

NAA-NAA
[mint tea]

'A gift from Allah' — the pervasive smell of mint tea, poured into
tall glasses and singing with an overdose of sugar, is the very essence
of Moroccan hospitality. It can be served cold, for those looking for
respite from the summer heat and the spiciness of the cuisine, or hot,
but always brimming with bristling fresh mint leaves which leap out
of the glass and wake the mind up to the mayhem of a Moroccan day.

rinse out a teapot with boiling water, add the green tea and then fill the pot with boiling water. allow the tea to steep for a few minutes. in serving glasses (tall clear ones are best), add sugar to taste — moroccans use at least one heaped tablespoon per person! add 4 or 5 sprigs of mint and half fill the glass with tea. stir to dissolve the sugar and at the same time push down on the mint, crushing the leaves. fill the glass with tea and serve immediately.

OPPOSITE: **char-grilled vegetables** [page 112], **couscous** [page 119], **harissa** [page 116]

FUL M'BAKHAR
[crunchy broad beans]

Serves 10

*500g (1lb) dried broad
beans, soaked overnight
in water to cover
(see note)
2 cups olive oil,
for deep-frying
4 cloves garlic, peeled
lekama (page 112)*

*No honest market haggler worth their spice salt would be caught
without a fresh helping of these little gems. As the 5am call to
prayer wafts through a crackling megaphone and the hooded faithful
quicken their stride, the early morning market is in full swing.
The trade is brisk but the normally hoarse vendors speak in whispered
tones, subdued by the reverential hour. A cup of freshly fried beans
tossed in a little spice salt and tipped into a pre-rolled newspaper cone
is in my hand before I can say 's'Allah malacum' — God be with you.
The vendor replies by reversing the sentence, and although it's not quite
dawn, I am able to make out the large toothless gaps in his smile.*

drain the beans and dry well. in a heavy-based saucepan, frying pan or wok, heat half the oil on high until it begins to smoke. carefully add half the beans and 2 whole garlic cloves to the oil and, with a slotted spoon or spatula, swirl the beans around so they fry evenly. if the oil continues to smoke, turn the heat down to medium. after a few minutes when the beans and garlic begin to turn golden, remove them with the slotted spoon and drain on paper towels. cook the next batch.

once most of the oil has been absorbed by the paper towels, toss the warm beans in **lekama** and serve immediately, or allow to cool and store in an airtight container for up to two days.

[
note: although chickpeas are commonly used in this manner, broad beans are particularly well suited because of their tendency to split, which helps maintain their crunch.

Also extremely popular is *bessara*, steamed broad beans that are blended to a paste with a little oil, garlic and lemon.
]

OPPOSITE: **enchiladas de arrachera al carbon en adobo** — chilli-dipped tortillas with char-grilled steak [page 135], and **salsa mexicana** — fresh tomato salsa [page 131]

4 parts salt
2 parts paprika
1 part ground cumin
1 part pepper
1 part ground coriander
1 part chilli powder

Serves 8

*2 each of the following
vegetables:
potatoes, yams, sweet
potatoes, carrots, turnips
and parsnips
(corn is also excellent)*
*¹/₂ cup olive oil,
for brushing*
lekama

LEKAMA
[spice salt]

Cumin, salt and pepper are the essentials to any **lekama**
*— a general term for seasoning in Morocco. Most street vendors offer
spice salt in tiny cones of newspaper, twisted at the top,
to allow their customers to add it at their own discretion.*

mix the ingredients together well and place in a salt shaker or bowl. spice salt will keep in an airtight container indefinitely, but will lose its potency once the spices are more than a few months old.

CHAR-GRILLED VEGETABLES

*Moroccans tend to choose vegetables high in starch, such as yams,
sweet potatoes (kumera) and turnips, for cooking over an open flame.
By parboiling them first and then grilling, the flesh becomes almost
creamy while the outside takes on a distinctive charcoal flavour.*

bring a large pot of lightly salted water to the boil and turn down the heat until the water is just simmering. cook the vegetables in batches. when there is still a little resistance if a wooden skewer is poked into the centre. remove from the pot and drain well.

brush the vegetables with a little olive oil and cook them in a char-grill pan or on the barbecue. turn once the skin starts to darken and cook the other side. remove, sprinkle with **lekama** and serve.

[**note:** a simple and delicious accompaniment can be created by adding a pinch of **lekama** to yoghurt or tahini thinned out with a little water and lemon juice.]

HARIRA
[moroccan soup]

A soup that breaks the fast after sunset and sustains the faith during
*Ramadan, **harira** is a symphony of homely nourishment and religious*
celebration. It is also a dish that lends itself to variations
depending on the whims of the cook and the bounty of the pantry.
At other times of the year it is served as a warming breakfast or
*lunchtime snack. In markets throughout Morocco, **harira** stalls*
are recognisable by their long tables and stacks of ceramic soup bowls.

Serves 6

1.5kg (3lb) chicken
2 tbsp butter
2 tbsp olive oil
2 large onions, sliced
4 cloves garlic, chopped
salt and freshly ground
black pepper, to taste
pinch of saffron or 1 tsp
ground turmeric
1 tsp cinnamon
2 large ripe tomatoes,
chopped
1 cup chickpeas, soaked
overnight in water to
cover then drained
1 cup short-grain rice
$^1/_2$ cup plain flour
dissolved in 1 cup water
and left overnight to sour
1 bunch parsley, chopped
2 eggs, beaten
3–4 lemons, quartered

place the chicken in a large, heavy-based saucepan, pour in water to cover and simmer until well cooked, about 1$^1/_2$ hours. (traditionally, the chicken, or even just the carcass, is left on the embers of the fire to simmer overnight.) remove the chicken, shred the meat from the bones and discard the carcass. strain the stock and set aside.

in a deep, heavy-based pot, heat the butter and oil and gently fry the onions and garlic until translucent. add the spices and tomatoes and simmer until the mixture has reduced to a thick sauce. add the chickpeas, rice and reserved chicken stock and simmer until the chickpeas are done, about 1 hour.

pour the flour and water mixture into the soup in a thin stream, stirring all the while. mix and continue to stir for 15 minutes. add the shredded chicken meat, just to warm through. remove from heat, add the parsley and then, stirring constantly, add the eggs in a thin stream. this completes the creaminess of the soup. allow to stand for a few minutes before serving with a generous squeeze of lemon juice.

OMELETTO
[prawn and almond omelette]

2 tbsp butter
$^1/_2$ cup flaked or slivered
almonds
4 cloves garlic, crushed
24 small uncooked
prawns, peeled
1 tsp ground coriander
1 tsp ground cumin
1 tsp paprika
1 tsp chilli powder
12 eggs beaten
with 1 tbsp water
2 tbsp chopped parsley
salt and freshly ground
black pepper
1 lemon, cut into wedges

*Mid-morning in the medina of Fez. The hawker's shrill cry tugged at
every ear attached to a craving stomach. He sported a nonchalant,
almost disdainful look and a well-groomed moustache.
'Om-e-letto! Om-e-letto!' he cried — but this was no ordinary
omelette. This guy knew what he was doing.
In minutes flat he created a beautifully light dish, studded with fresh
prawns and completed with the nuttiness of seared almonds.*

heat a wok or large frying pan on high heat and add $^1/_2$ tablespoon butter immediately followed by $^1/_4$ of the almonds. stir for 1 minute, then add $^1/_4$ of the garlic and 6 or so prawns. stir-fry for a few minutes until the prawns turn pink, then add a pinch of each spice. when fragrant, add $^1/_4$ of the beaten egg mix, swirl it around the pan until the bottom has just set, then tear a few holes and lift the omelette slightly to let the uncooked eggs run underneath. turn the heat right down, sprinkle over a quarter of the parsley, season to taste with salt and pepper and cover with a lid. after a few minutes the omelette will be set — don't overcook it! it's vital to cook the eggs only to the point where they are just set.

tip the wok and gently slide half the omelette onto a plate, then fold the remaining half over the top with a spatula. cover with a tea towel and keep warm. repeat the procedure and make three more omelettes. serve with a wedge of lemon.

L'MAH HARH
[steamed clams]

Serves 6

*As the sun sets over the Atlas ranges, the red ochre of the buildings
in Marrakech's Jamna El F'Na glow to a point of near fluorescence.
Street entertainers vie for a few shekels, and their conjuring call is
highlighted by the swirling steam and aromas that arise from the
cauldrons of the food hawkers. Bowls of steaming broth from the
clam stalls are served to whoever sits at the communal tables that lie
like a confused game of dominoes across the square.*

*$1/_2$ cup olive oil
2kg (4 lb) clams (pippies)
or mussels
8 cloves garlic, crushed
1 tbsp finely chopped red
chilli
1 tbsp ground cumin
1 tbsp paprika
1 tsp cayenne
salt and freshly ground
black pepper, to taste
1 bunch parsley,
chopped, plus extra
2 cups water
2 lemons, cut into
wedges*

heat the olive oil in a heavy-based saucepan until very hot and add the clams in batches
to cover the bottom of the pan in one layer — don't add too many at once. cover and
shake the pan until the clams open. add the garlic, chilli, spices and parsley, and cook,
stirring, for a few minutes, then add the water. once it has come to the boil, remove from
heat and serve immediately with wedges of lemon and a sprinkling of parsley.

HARISSA
[red chilli paste]

Makes about 1 cup

*250g (8oz) fresh red
chillies, finely chopped
(see note)
12 large cloves garlic,
chopped
1 tbsp salt
1 tbsp coriander seeds
1 tbsp cumin seeds
2 tbsp olive oil
(approximately)
1/2 bunch mint leaves
1 bunch coriander,
roots only
juice and peel of 2
lemons*

*No Moroccan street vendor, restaurant chef or home cook would dare
be caught without their own version of this fiery relish. Some would
argue that the omission of tomato flesh, black pepper, fresh ginger or
cardamom seeds from the following recipe amounts to culinary
sacrilege. A staple condiment, often used as a basis for marinades,
the tiniest teaspoon of* **harissa** *will lift the flavour of any dish
... as well as the roof of your mouth.*

traditionally the paste is ground in a mortar and pestle, a process that helps to release the flavour from the ingredients. if that sounds like too much hard work, a food processor will do the job quickly and easily.

if using a food processor, first fry the chillies, garlic and spices in a little oil to bring out the flavour. place all the ingredients in the food processor and blend to a paste. transfer the **harissa** to a jar and cover with a thin layer of olive oil. keeps indefinitely in the refrigerator, as long as it is always covered by a thin layer of oil.

[**note**: if a less than ballistic heat is desired, cut the chillies in half, discard the seeds and white membrane, and soak in water for 30 minutes.]

L'HOOTZ MISCHUI
[barbecued fish kebabs]

cut the fish into 3cm (1^1/$_4$in) cubes. cut the peppers and onion into 3cm (1^1/$_4$in) squares. combine the remaining ingredients and pour into a baking dish. thread the skewers with fish cubes interspersed with capsicum and onion, and place them in the baking dish to marinate for 30 minutes. grill for a few minutes on all sides, basting frequently with the marinade. serve with **schlada dsjada** , plain white rice or couscous.

Serves 4

1kg (2lb) firm white fish fillets
2 green peppers
2 red peppers
1 large onion
^{1}/$_2$ cup olive oil
juice of 2 lemons
1 tbsp **harissa**
(recipe opposite)
^{1}/$_2$ cup chopped coriander leaves
salt and freshly ground black pepper

12 wooden skewers, soaked in water for 1 hour

SCHLADA DSJADA
[carrot salad]

Tangiers is a port city of ill repute — a mixture of the seedy and the seductive. The narrow cobbled streets are surely created to confuse the foreigner. As the shadows and unfamiliar sounds fuelled my paranoia, I was saved (or 'kidnapped' — I never quite worked out which) by an overenthusiastic restaurant proprietor. The establishment was not well lit and as I had not been forewarned about the chilli assault known as **harissa**, *misfortune was just a matter of time. To douse the fire (i.e. after the rollicking laughter abated), the host prepared in seconds flat a salad that seemed little more than grated carrot. Ah! But the relief. The sweet, cooling side-dish took immediate effect and I was forever after ordering* **schlada dsjada** *with every meal.*

first, toast the pine nuts. either spread them out on a baking tray and place in a hot oven until browned, or toss them in an unoiled wok over high heat. when cool, mix together all the ingredients in a large bowl. check for seasoning and serve.

[**note:** make sure you have all the ingredients ready so the salad can be thrown together just prior to serving. the carrots must be crisp and fresh and should never be grated and left for more than 15 minutes.]

Serves 4

2 tbsp pine nuts
4 medium carrots (small carrots are sweetest), peeled and grated
2 tbsp poppy seeds
1 clove garlic, crushed
2 tbsp olive oil
2 tbsp white vinegar
1 tbsp chopped mint
salt and freshly ground black pepper

117

HAMID MSYIAR

[preserved lemons]

An absolute necessity if you want to get serious about Moroccan cuisine.

a couple of large pickling jars
2kg (4lb) ripe lemons
150g (5oz) ground sea salt

sterilise the jars with boiling water and allow to drip dry. wash the lemons and slice them lengthwise into quarters, but do not cut right through — leave the quarters attached at the stem end. rub plenty of salt into the lemons and place them in the jars, pressing down firmly with a heavy weight such as a well washed stone to release their juices (it is the released juices that preserve the lemons).

add extra lemon juice or water to cover, if necessary. seal the jars and store in a warm place (but not in direct sunlight). don't worry if you notice some spots of mould — that's quite normal. simply empty the jars and clean them out, then return the lemons and juice. store for a minimum of 3 weeks before using. the lemons will keep for 6–8 weeks.

COUSCOUS

Without doubt, the most widely known food in Moroccan cuisine is couscous. (The original name suksoo proved a bit too much of a mouthful for the French colonists.) The couscous grain is a yellow-gold colour and is made from durum wheat semolina. The traditional method for making couscous is time-consuming, and many Moroccans buy it from those whose reputations result from a lifetime of dedication to the cause. Pre-prepared authentic grains can be purchased from specialty grocery stores and the effort is well worth it, as the instant couscous available from most supermarkets is passable but in no way resembles the soft, fluffy grains that Moroccans swoon over. Couscous is almost always served as a bed for a **tagine** or stew, two classic versions of which follow. For this reason the couscous should be steamed over the pot (ideally in a traditional couscousier) in which the stew is cooking for about 1 hour. This allows the flavour of the stock to permeate the couscous. Couscous is also the name of the traditional Moroccan dish which, like pilaf from the Middle East and biriyani from the Indian subcontinent, is a meal in itself. It makes a stunning centrepiece to a Moroccan-style buffet. Try tossing freshly prepared couscous with toasted pine nuts, raisins, roast capsicums and parsley. Mound on a serving platter and serve with a salad for a light and delicious lunch. There are sweet versions of couscous, too, which are similar to baked rice desserts such as the Greek risogolo (see **couscous sffa'** on page 122). If using instant couscous, follow the packet directions. If you manage to get your hands on authentic couscous, simply spread out in a steamer, place over the pot in which the tagine is cooking, cover tightly and steam for approximately 1 hour, or until the grains are soft yet still maintain their shape. In either case, before serving, fluff the couscous with a fork and enrich it with a sprinkling of virgin olive oil or a few dabs of butter.

1kg (2lb) fish steaks
(kingfish, cod or bream)
1 preserved lemon
1 cup water

CHERMOULA
4 tbsp olive oil
2 onions, chopped
6 cloves garlic, finely
chopped
2 tsp ground cumin
1 tsp ground turmeric
1 tsp salt
1 green pepper, sliced
12 spanish black or
kalamata olives
1/2 bunch coriander,
chopped

TAGINE BE L'HOOTZ
[fish stew]

*Chermoula is an almost-dry marinade that is transferred to the
cooking vessel and forms the basis of the stew. Unlike dishes where
the marinade is discarded before cooking, or used to baste grilled
food, with chermoula nothing is wasted and it is essential to
the flavour of the tangine.*

mix together the chermoula ingredients and place a third of the mixture on the bottom of a large ceramic baking dish. arrange the fish steaks in a single layer on top. pull the preserved lemon apart with your fingers and tuck it under the fish. pour over the rest of the chermoula and leave to marinate for at least 4 hours or overnight in the fridge, turning occasionally.

preheat the oven to 180°C (350°F). pour the water over the fish and cover with a lid or tightly fitted foil. cook for 15–20 minutes. the fish is ready when it's just beginning to flake at its thickest part. remove from heat and, with the lid on, allow the fish to continue steaming for a further 5 minutes. serve straight from the baking dish or piled on a mountain of freshly steamed **couscous** (page 119).

TAGINE GNAOUA
[gnaouan vegetable stew]

Serves 4–6

The Gnaouans are of Berber origin, renowned for the passion with which they embrace their music. The trance-like state induced through song and dance is said to transport them to a place where the heart is pure and they are blessed with mystical powers to see into the future. As the tempo intensifies, the Gnaouans, in their bare feet and embroidered tunics, gyrate and pulsate in a frenzy of rhythm and colour. While poverty may have dictated their diet, they have an abundance of energy and enthusiasm — the Gnaouans are champions of packing flavour and vitality into their vegetable tagines. Part of the attraction of this dish is the way the softer vegetables disintegrate, thickening the sauce.

2 tbsp olive oil
2 onions, chopped
4 cloves garlic, chopped
1 tbsp paprika
1 tsp cumin seeds
2 cups chickpeas, soaked overnight in water to cover then drained
2 tbsp chopped parsley
2 carrots, chopped
1 turnip, chopped
2 medium potatoes, cubed
1 medium eggplant, cubed
1 large squash or zucchini, cut into 1cm ($^1/_3$in) rounds
2 cups water
salt and freshly ground black pepper
1 lemon, cut into quarters
extra chopped parsley

heat the olive oil in a large saucepan over medium heat and fry the onions and garlic until translucent. stir in the paprika and cumin seeds and continue stirring until the seeds have popped, taking care that the paprika doesn't stick to the bottom of the pan — add a little water if necessary. stir in the chickpeas, coating them with the spices. pour in enough water to cover and cook, covered, until the liquid has reduced to a thick sauce.

add the parsley, carrots, turnip, potatoes, eggplant, squash and water. bring to the boil, then simmer until all the vegetables are tender. add salt and pepper to taste and remove from heat. just prior to serving, squeeze lemon juice over the **tagine** and sprinkle with some additional parsley. serve with freshly steamed **couscous** (page 119).

1/2 cup sugar
2 cups water
6 quinces, peeled and
quartered
1 stick cinnamon

COUSCOUS
2 tbsp butter
1/2 cup pine nuts
250g (8oz) couscous
pinch of salt
1/3 cup sugar
or 2 tbsp honey
1/2 cup raisins

COUSCOUS SFFA'
[sweet couscous with quince, pine nuts and raisins]

QUINCES: in a heavy-based saucepan, dissolve the sugar in the water. add the quince quarters and the stick of cinnamon, cover and simmer for 15–20 minutes. to check the quince is cooked, insert a wooden skewer into the middle — there should be no resistance at all. (some cooks prefer their quince to be mushy like a thick sauce, but personally I find a little texture is preferable). remove from heat and set aside.

COUSCOUS: melt the butter over low heat, add the pine nuts and fry until golden. set aside. if using instant couscous, mix with the salt and sugar or honey, pour in boiling water just to cover and steam for 15 minutes. (if using authentic couscous, steam over a pot of water as described on page 119. while hot, mix in the salt, sugar or honey). stir in the butter and pine nut mixture, reserving some pine nuts for garnish, and fluff the couscous with a fork. mix in the raisins; the heat and moisture will cause them to swell, so there's no need to soak them first. check for seasoning — it shouldn't be too sweet. set aside.

put a few scoops of couscous onto each plate and spoon 3–4 slices of quince and some of the sweet juice on top. sprinkle with the remaining pine nuts and serve. a swirl of pouring cream or condensed milk can also be used as a garnish.

M'KULI

[chicken with preserved lemons and olives]

Serves 4

On the west coast of Morocco, a decaying Portuguese fort gazes out
at the Atlantic like a forlorn sentinel. The town of Essaouira
grew around and gradually transformed the relics of an empire
into a sanctuary for local artists.
The air is filled with the scent of freshly turned wood mixed with the
sea spray that drifts over the fortress wall. I spent many hours here,
sipping mint tea with the artists, admiring the quality of their work
and sharing the enthusiasm with which they embrace life. It was just a
stone's throw away from my favourite street-side cafe, Mama's.
They told me Jimmy Hendrix had eaten here. They swore Bob Dylan
had shared their hookah pipe and Cat Stevens did a jig on the table.
(As it turns out, every cafe in town has been blessed by one patron
saint of sixties psychedelia). While I strummed a beaten-up Spanish
guitar, Mama — one hundred or so kilograms of pure black African
mischief — did the dance of m'kuli *to rid the world*
(or at least hordes of locals) of famine.

2 large onions, sliced
4 cloves garlic, chopped
5cm (2in) piece ginger,
julienned
2 tbsp olive oil
1 tsp ground turmeric
1 tsp ground cumin
1.5kg (1lb) chicken, cut
into 8 pieces
(see note)
1 tsp thyme
1 tbsp plain flour
(optional)
1 cup water
1 preserved lemon, cut
into 2mm ($^1/_8$in) strips
$^1/_2$ cup spanish black
olives
salt and freshly ground
black pepper
2 tbsp chopped parsley

in a heavy-based frying pan, gently sauté the onions, garlic and ginger in olive oil until the onions are translucent. stir in the turmeric and cumin and fry until fragrant. add the chicken pieces, turning frequently to coat with the spices. when lightly browned, add the thyme. if a thick sauce is desired, sprinkle over the flour and continue to stir for a few minutes while the flour cooks and blends with the spices.

pour in enough water to cover, add the preserved lemon and the olives, and season with salt and pepper. lower the heat to a gentle simmer and cover with a lid. cook for 25–30 minutes or until the chicken is tender. garnish with chopped parsley and serve with plain white rice or **couscous** (page 119).

note: keep the chicken pieces on the bone; they add flavour to the stock and thicken the sauce with the release of gelatin. moroccans wouldn't dare dispense with the lip-smacking, slurping ecstasy of sucking the meat from the bone.

SESAME GINGER SNAPS

Makes 30

4 cups honey
3 cups sesame seeds
$1/2$ tsp ground ginger
peanut oil

Moroccans love sweets and, in the larger markets, just about anything
is fair prey to be doused in a cloyingly sweet syrup.
Perhaps the all-time favourite is **shebbakia,** *a deep-fried ribbon of*
pastry, soaked in honey and dipped in sesame seeds. However,
it is a little too heavy and oily for many foreigners, so here is
another popular treat, the sesame snap.

for this recipe, use a heavy-based saucepan with very deep sides, as the honey can bubble over. heat the honey on low, stirring constantly, until it reaches the 'hard crack' or candy stage. this will take about 50–60 minutes. stir in the sesame seeds and ginger and allow to cool for a few minutes.

lightly oil a 40cm x 30cm (16in x 12in) baking tray. pour in the sesame and honey mixture and leave to cool. before it sets completely, score the top in a criss-cross pattern or diamond shape. when completely cool, separate the pieces and store in an airtight container.

Mexico

Mexico is the eccentric uncle of this book.
It possesses a remarkable cuisine – each recipe, far from being an end in itself, is a building block, an open invitation to both subtle variation and wild experimentation.

La Merced, the market in Mexico City is testimony to this. More like a metropolis than a market with its 600 blocks of fresh produce (five square blocks of sweets alone!), it provides a lifestyle for thousands and feeds one of the largest cities in the world. The amazing fresh fruit section comprises a large proportion of the market with row upon row of stalls with magnificently tiered displays – a precarious balance that tempts the hungry *gringo* to bring down the entire exhibit. Tropical fruits from the south, enormous mangoes, ruby-red papayas (pawpaws) and a dozen different kinds of bananas rub shoulders with products from the arid north, including cactus flowers and every variety of nut imaginable. There is an entire section devoted to the dried chilli – over two blocks! - just for the population to satiate their penchant for heat. And still another section is dedicated to the 'weird and wonderful' tastes that are meekly described as authentic, indigenous or traditional Mexican specialities – pickled iguana, deep-fried grasshopper, spiced turtle and so on. (I can testify to crispy grasshopper as a superb accompaniment to a really cold bear – and it makes for great conversation piece to

boot). All this and I and I haven't even mentioned the incredible variety of street stalls that cater for the ravenous shoppers and vendors alike – *taquerias* are lined up for hundreds of metres, there are dozens of *licuados* (fruit drink) vendors, *chicharrones* (crispy pork rind) makers and soup stalls of every description. La Merced has claim to being the largest market of its type in the world and, as such, it is a living museum of the versatility and vitality of street food.

I spent several days wandering around and sampling the fare. Street food vendors in Mexico, just like those in Southeast Asia, are wily and proud folk who know their strength lies in being able to execute one specialty better than anyone else. And so it was with the **tortilla** stalls, where rows of furiously diligent women slaved over the **tortilla** presses, either selling a few to the hunched grandmothers on their way back to the family home, or in bulk to the **burrito** stands that operate within a handshake of each other. Immense griddles, large enough to spread out three or four **tortillas** at a time, are surrounded by neatly arranged containers of every ingredient imaginable. Many are raw, such as a selection of freshly chopped chillies, others are pre-prepared, such as steamed mushrooms or shredded chicken. You simply call out your fillings of choice and within seconds the assembling is completed and your **tortilla** is singing away on the griddle.

Mexico wouldn't be Mexico without the **tortilla**. Generally speaking, the difference between the three Ts – **tortillas**, **tacos** and **tostadas** – is in size, method of assembly and whether corn or wheat flour is used. However, there are no steadfast rules. **Tortillas** resemble large, soft, flat bread, **tacos** are smaller and are first filled with the improvised delights of the day, then folded or fried, and **tostadas** are smaller still, fried crisp and then piled high with a multitude of fresh ingredients – much like an open sandwich.

With the Tropic of Cancer carving Mexico neatly in half, it would seem easy to separate the country into climatically dictated zones – from the southern tropics to the temperate north – yet Mexico also includes great expanses of desert, magnificent beaches, highlands of bitter cool and areas of near impenetrable jungle. As expected, this leads to some variation in the types of food available and while common elements that bind the country are never far from sight, it is regional specialities that make Mexican cuisine such an enjoyable discovery. Right throughout the nation, the mix of *indigena*, Spanish and, to a much lesser degree, French influences, are sewn into the fabric of Mexican cuisine. Almost all Mexicans take their main meal of the day, *comida*, between two and four in the afternoon. This can be a set meal, *comida corrida*, or *a la carte* – both feature several courses that enforce a siesta afterwards. Dinner is usually taken quite late and is a much lighter meal comprising of a soup or a variety of snacks.

The most common ingredients that go into Mexican cooking generally depend on what part of the country you are in. Corn is everywhere and is the staple base for **tortillas**. Ground spiced beef or pork is exceptionally popular. Seafood, particularly prawns and fish, is common in the coastal areas, while *pollo* (chicken), *huevos* (eggs), *hongos* (mushrooms), *frijoles refritos* (refried beans) and a multitude of *moles* and *salsas* (sauces) bring every dish an invigorating lift. Along with chocolate and vanilla, Mexico introduced the chilli to the rest of the world and thus brought a common misconception that all Mexican food is hot. This is not the case and it totally depends on the individual as to how much chilli one wants – most truly hot sauces are served separately for use at the consumer's discretion. So any culinary nuclear fission depends entirely on how you like it.

Drinking makes up a large part of Mexican social life, particularly for the men. *Cantinas* are all-male domains and once you step inside, it is an unspoken agreement that you will not leave the same way. A drink with a Mexican can be a serious affair – much machismo rides on matching each other drink for drink – and their choice of poison is deadly. *Mezcal* is a distilled alcohol from the maguey plant and its infamous cousin, *tequila*, from a region of the same name, tend to take hold of the senses and not let go. Mexican beer is exceptionally good and much lighter than most brands in the west – with a wedge of lime squeezed into the bottle and salt pressed over the rim, you have a true Mexican experience.

The history of Mexico is one of violent upheavals, soaring empires and tragic defeats. The great Mayan Empire (300-900 AD) whose architectural genius continues to inspire designers today, left behind a series of majestic cities that now lie in ruins in Chiapas and the Yucatan Peninsula. With all their wealth in mathematics, engineering, astronomy and the creative arts, scientists are still dumbfounded as to the cause of their demise – their apparent inability to feed themselves.

In central Mexico one of the greatest architectural sites, the city of Teo*tihuacan*, rises from the plain as a solemn reminder – yet another ancient sentinel to the story of a society collapsed. Standing atop the Pyramid of the Moon and peering through the dry heat haze of a Mexican afternoon at *Calle De Los Muertos* (Road of the Dead), one feels giddy at the contemplation of what befell such an empire. Not even the Aztecs could figure who built such a stirring metropolis – they believed it was the work of giants and went on to construct Tenochitlan 50 kilometres (30 miles) away, a city of such magnificence that reports filed back in Europe spoke of a 'Venice of the New World'. The *Chinampas* or Floating Gardens, were a wonder of beauty and turned the previous swamp into the arable land that former *empires* had so desperately needed.

Through the latter half of the twentieth century, Mexico has continued to suffer at the hands of internal despots and external imperialists – many Mexicans have a cynical eye when it comes to both foreign powers and national governments. As a country made up of very distinct cultural regions, unity is often questioned when it infringes on cultural differences. So just as the people of any religion are proud and passionate about their history, their regional crafts and the beauty of their landscape, the best way they know of treating you to a unique experience is to take you to an eatery that specialises in local cuisine, fill your belly to the brim and then afterwards to a *cantina* to get plastered. Mexican hospitality is dangerously exuberant.

The following recipes are just a few suggested combinations and a handful of the myriad sauces and accompaniments that go into making Mexican cuisine so special. Feel free to experiment and invent your own combinations.

TORTILLAS
[griddle-baked bread]

*Makes 12 **tortillas***

*Essentially, a griddle is a hot plate, usually of slightly concave, tempered cast-iron. These days, machines are becoming increasingly popular, putting out of business the operators of traditional **tortilla** presses — a hinged two-sided griddle that resembles a waffle iron without the corrugations.*

3 cups masa harina *(fine cornmeal) or plain flour*
1 tsp salt
$^1/_2$ cup lard
1 cup hot water

mix together the flour, salt and lard in a large mixing bowl until well combined. pour in the water a little at a time and mix with a spatula or fork. when all the dry ingredients are moistened (it's important not to use too much water as the dough will not hold together), knead the dough on a lightly floured surface for at least 10 minutes, or until the dough is smooth. divide into 12 equal balls, cover with plastic wrap and rest for 30 minutes.

place each ball on a well-floured surface and use a rolling pin to roll them into disks about 20cm (8in) in diameter. heat a large, ungreased heavy-based frying pan over medium heat but do not oil. cook the tortillas one at a time, about 30 seconds each side, until spotted with brown, about 30–45 seconds. stack the tortillas on top of each other as you go, keeping them covered with a tea towel to stop them drying out.

1¹/₂ tbsp vegetable oil
1 onion, chopped
2 cloves garlic, chopped
500g (1lb) minced pork
1 stick cinnamon
pinch of ground cloves
salt and freshly ground
black pepper
2 x 400g (12oz) cans
peeled tomatoes, pureed
juice of 1 lime
¹/₄ cup raisins
¹/₄ cup silvered almonds

TORTILLAS CON PICADILLO OAXAQUENO

[tortillas with minced pork, almonds and raisins]

The combination of almonds and raisins with pork
makes this a really tasty dish, slightly sweet yet with a savoury bite.

heat the oil in a frying pan over medium heat and cook the onion until soft, then add the garlic. after a few minutes, add the pork and cook, stirring, until slightly browned. add the spices to the pan, season to taste with salt and pepper, then add the tomatoes, lime juice and raisins. simmer until the mixture is the texture of thick gravy, about 45 minutes.

toast the almonds for a few minutes and stir them into the mixture.

serve in a bowl with warm **tortillas** (page 129) and a choice of accompaniments: for example, **salsa verde cruda**, some *queso fresco* (a mexican-style mozzarella) or grated cheddar and a bowl of *crema espesa*.

[
note: the nearest approximation to mexican *crema espesa* can be obtained by thinning a cup of sour cream with 2 tablespoons of milk. alternatively use french *crème fraîche*.
]

Makes about 4 cups

15 fresh tomatillos
(mexican green
tomatoes), husked and
washed
or 2 x 400g (12oz)
cans tomatillos
1 clove garlic, chopped
¹/₂ white onion, chopped
¹/₂ cup roughly chopped
coriander leaves
2–3 green serrano
chillies, seeded
¹/₂ tsp salt

SALSA VERDE CRUDA

[fresh green tomatillo sauce]

bring a pot of water to the boil and boil the fresh tomatillos for 7–8 minutes. set aside to cool. (if using canned tomatillos, this step is not necessary.) place the remaining ingredients in a food processor or blender and blend to a paste. add the tomatillos and half a cup of their cooking liquid and pulse to a coarse puree. the salsa will keep for up to 1 week in the refrigerator.

SALSA PICANTE
[hot sauce]

You want to breathe fire like the rancheros? This is the salsa that will do it, so take care! However, there's no shame in lessening the heat if you so desire; just reduce the number of chillies and leave the perspiring

to the hardened chilli-muncher.

10 plum tomatoes or
3 large round
tomatoes, halved
40 dried anchos chillies,
seeded
$1/2$ tsp cumin seeds
1 tbsp sesame seeds
2 tbsp pumpkin seeds
4 allspice berries
1 tsp salt
3 cloves garlic, chopped
1 tsp dried oregano
$1/2$ cup cider vinegar

place the tomatoes cut-side down on a sheet of aluminium foil and cook under a very hot grill for 15 minutes. reserve the juices. peel off the blackened skin and discard. place the tomato flesh and chillies in a food processor or blender.

heat a heavy-based frying pan on low and cook the cumin and sesame seeds, stirring constantly until they brown, then add them to the tomatoes and chillies in the blender. do the same with the pumpkin seeds. crack the allspice berries and add them to the blender with the salt, garlic, oregano and vinegar. pulse until the mixture is well combined but has a slightly lumpy texture.

serve immediately or transfer to an airtight container and store in the refrigerator for up to 2 weeks.

SALSA MEXICANA
[fresh tomato salsa]

Makes about 2 cups

An all-purpose, zippy salsa that, like frijoles refritos,

should be at hand whenever there's a Mexican morsel to be had.

2 large ripe tomatoes,
cored and chopped
1 white onion, diced
1 clove garlic, crushed
2 jalapeño chillies, finely
sliced
juice of 1 lime
$1/2$ tsp salt
$1/4$ cup chopped coriander
1 tbsp water

combine all the ingredients in a bowl and let stand for 30 minutes.

Makes 3 cups

1 white onion, finely
chopped
1 large ripe tomato,
cored and finely chopped
$1/4$ cup chopped
coriander leaves
2 green serrano chillies,
finely chopped
1 clove garlic, crushed
juice of 1 lime
salt and freshly ground
black pepper
3 large, ripe avocados

GUACAMOLE
[avocado salsa]

Everyone claims that they make the best **guacamole**.
Ultimately it's down to personal taste — some prefer mashed avocado
with a little lemon juice, others pack in as many ingredients
as they can muster. For me a great 'guac' relies on beautifully
ripe avocados and the slightly sweet tartness of lime
... but millions of Mexicans would disagree.

guacamole is best made just prior to serving, so prepare the ingredients, reserving a little onion, tomato and coriander for garnish.

combine the onion, tomato, coriander, chillies, garlic, lime juice and a pinch of salt and pepper in a serving bowl. cut the avocados in half. discard the stone, mash the flesh roughly with a fork and fold it into the ingredients in the bowl. garnish with the reserved onion, tomato and coriander and serve.

TACOS CON POLLO Y SALSA PICANTE

[soft tortilla roll-ups with chicken in a spicy sauce]

Serves 6

put the onion, garlic, bay leaves, salt and water into saucepan and bring to a simmer. add the chicken and cook gently until almost done, about 10–12 minutes. leave the chicken in the stock and set aside to cool. once cool, tear the chicken into 3–4cm (1$^1/_4$–1$^1/_2$in) long shreds. place the shredded chicken in a bowl with just enough stock to keep the chicken moist.

meanwhile, to make the **tacos**, follow the method for making **tortillas** on page 129, except break the dough into 18 equal balls and roll into discs about 5cm in diameter. keep the **tacos** warm by standing them on a hot plate and wrapping them in a tea towel.

to serve, line a **taco** with some shredded lettuce, add a tablespoon of chicken, drizzle over some **sauce picante** and finish with a generous dollop of **guacamole**.

CHICKEN
1 onion, cut in half
1 clove garlic, peeled
2 bay leaves
1 tsp salt
2 cups water
2 large chicken breasts,
cut in half

TACOS
3 cups masa harina
(cornmeal) or plain flour
1 tsp salt
$^1/_2$ cup lard
1 cup hot water

TO SERVE
shredded lettuce
salsa picante
(page 131)
guacamole
(recipe opposite)

4 chorizo sausages

TO BOIL THE BEANS
2 cups pinto or black
beans, soaked overnight
in water to cover and
drained
2 tbsp lard
1 onion, chopped
6 cups water
(approximately)
1 tbsp salt

TO REFRY THE
BEANS
4 tbsp lard
1 onion, finely chopped
2 cloves garlic, crushed
3 cups cooked beans,
plus broth
salt and freshly ground
black pepper

TOSTADAS
3 cups masa harina
(cornmeal) or plain flour
1 tsp salt
1/2 cup lard
1 cup hot water

TO SERVE
shredded lettuce
slices of tomato
guacamole *(page 132)*

TOSTADAS CON CHORIZIO Y FRIJOLES REFRITOS

[crisp-fried mini tortillas with spicy sausage and refried beans]

In many of the central plazas throughout Mexico, **tostadas** *carts are lined up, jostling for a superior position in which to lure customers.*

Condiments surround stacks of crispy, golden **tostadas.**

Wickedly rich, chorizo is a spicy sausage made from fatty pork.

It's a flavour-boosting addition to any dish,

served with plenty of rice, potatoes or bread.

Refried beans accompany almost every Mexican meal — you must specify if you don't want them on your plate. They serve as lubricators — much healthier than butter, and delicious on their own.

remove the outer casing from the chorizo and cut the sausage into bite-sized chunks. gently fry over low heat in an ungreased frying pan, stirring constantly, until browned. drain on paper towels and set aside.

TO BOIL THE BEANS: rinse the beans several times under running water, then place in a large saucepan with the lard and onion, pour in water to cover and simmer for 1 hour. add the salt and continue cooking for another hour, or until the beans are tender.

TO REFRY THE BEANS: heat the lard in a large, heavy-based saucepan and fry the onion and garlic until browned. add the beans 1 cup at a time, plus a little of the cooking broth, and mash with a wooden spoon or fork. keep stirring to prevent the beans sticking to the bottom of the pan. when the beans are a thick paste, season to taste with salt and pepper, remove from heat and cover.

TO MAKE THE TOSTADAS: follow the method for making **tortillas** on page 129, except break the dough into 24 equal portions and roll into thin discs about 10cm (4in) in diameter. fry until crisp, then drain on paper towels. when cool, briefly refry the **tostadas**, drain and sprinkle with a little salt.

TO SERVE: spread the **tostdas** with refried beans and top with shredded lettuce, pieces of chorizo, a slice of tomato and a dollop of **guacamole**.

ENCHILADAS DE ARRACHERA AL CARBON EN ADOBO

[chilli-dipped tortillas with char-grilled steak in a rich red chilli sauce]

Enchiladas *are corn* **tortillas** *dipped in a chilli sauce, fried and then rolled. The classic version is* enchilada verde, *which you can assemble using the chicken as described in the* **taco** *recipe (page 133) and the* **salsa verde** *(page 130). The variation that follows comes from a stall which was directly below my hotel window in Mexico City*

— a totally irresistible form of advertising!

marinate the steak in lime juice, oil, salt and pepper for at least 3 hours. reserve the marinade. grill the meat for 2–3 minutes on each side until medium–rare and set aside.

SAUCE: heat half the lard in a heavy-based frying pan and quickly fry the chillies until dark red. transfer to a food processor or blender. put the onion and garlic in the pan and cook until lightly browned, then add the cumin seeds and sugar. when the seeds have popped, add the mixture to the chillies and puree. heat the remaining lard and fry the chilli mixture until it is a thick, dark red paste. add the reserved marinade, beef stock, herbs and orange juice and simmer for up to 1 hour and remove from heat.

dip the **tortillas** in the sauce and quickly fry for a few seconds each side. stack on top of each other and cover with a warm tea towel. slice the reserved meat thinly across the grain, place on a hot plate and pour over some hot sauce.

TO SERVE: line the **tortillas** with a little shredded lettuce, a couple spoonfuls of the sauced steak, some onion, orange slices and green olives, and a drizzle of *crema*. roll up and eat immediately.

Serves 6

1kg (2lb) skirt steak,
trimmed of fat
juice of 4 limes
2 tbsp olive oil
salt and freshly ground
black pepper

SAUCE
4 tbsp lard
10 dried ancho chillies,
seeded
1 onion, chopped
3 cloves garlic
1 tsp cumin seeds
1 tbsp sugar
2 cups beef stock
1/2 tsp dried oregano
1/2 tsp dried thyme
1 bay leaf
1 cup orange juice

12 uncooked corn
tortillas *(page 129)*

TO SERVE
shredded lettuce
onion rings
orange slices
green olives
crema espesa

Serves 6

QUESADILLAS CON HONGAS AL VAPOR

[cheese-filled tortillas with 'steamed' mushrooms]

FILLING
2 tbsp lard
1 onion, chopped
3 cloves garlic, chopped
500g (1lb) button
mushrooms, sliced
salt and freshly ground
black pepper
1 jalapeño chilli, sliced
2 tbsp chopped oregano

12 uncooked corn
tortillas *(page 129)*

2 cups queso fresco
(see glossary) or grated
cheddar

2 cups vegetable oil,
for deep-frying

Quesadillas *are corn* **tortilla** *pockets which are almost always filled with cheese (hence* quesa) *and sometimes other taco-style fillings. They are then deep-fried and eaten piping hot with a selection of condiments such as* **guacamole** *or* **salsa mexicana.**

heat the lard in a heavy-based frying pan and gently fry the onion and garlic until soft. add the mushrooms, season to taste with salt and pepper and simmer for 15 minutes. remove from heat and stir in the chilli and oregano.

smooth 2 tablespoons of the filling across the centre of each **tortilla**, sprinkle with cheese and fold in half, pinching the edges together to form a tight seal.

heat the vegetable oil in a heavy-based saucepan until very hot and fry each **quesadilla** for a few minutes on each side until golden brown. drain on paper towels and keep warm in a low oven (150ºC/300ºF) until ready to serve.

BURRITOS CON CAMARONES EN SALSA DE CHIPOTLE
[wheat-flour tortillas with prawns in a chipotle sauce]

Serves 6

Burritos *are wheat flour* **tortillas** *that originated in the north of Mexico. This is a coastal variation using one of the most popular sauces from the port of Veracruz.*

place the prawns in a bowl, season with salt and pepper and pour in the lime juice. set aside to marinate for up to 1 hour.

place the tomatoes cut-side down on a sheet of aluminium foil and cook under a very hot grill for 15 minutes. reserve the juices. peel off the blackened skin and discard.

place the tomatoes and juices, chillies, garlic, onion, cloves, cinnamon, oregano and thyme in a blender or food processor. blend to a coarse puree.

heat the olive oil in a heavy-based frying pan and stir-fry the prawns until pink. remove to a plate and set aside. put the blended mixture into the pan and cook, stirring, for 5 minutes. add the white wine and reduce until the sauce is quite thick. return the prawns to the mixture and cook for a further 2 minutes.

to serve, line the **burritos** with shredded lettuce. spoon some prawn mixture down the middle, sprinkle over some *queso fresco* if desired, then roll up the **burrito**. serve with a puree of **guacamole** thinned out with a little pouring cream (you can omit the tomatoes) and pour over the **burritos**. finish off with some **salsa mexicana**.

1kg (2lb) uncooked prawns, peeled and deveined
salt and freshly ground black pepper
juice of 3 limes
10 plum tomatoes or 4 round tomatoes, halved
6 dried chipotle chillies, seeded
2 cloves garlic, chopped
1 onion, chopped
2 whole cloves
5cm (2in) stick cinnamon, broken into pieces
1 tsp dried oregano
1 tsp thyme
$1/4$ cup olive oil
$1/2$ cup dry white wine

12 wheat-flour tortillas, wrapped in a warm tea towel (use the recipe on page 129 substituting plain flour for the masa harina)

shredded lettuce
queso fresco
guacamole *(page 132)*
salsa mexicana
(page 131)

DOUGH
4 cups boiling water
500g (1lb) coarse
semolina
500g (1lb) masa harina
(cornmeal)
1 tsp baking powder
1 cup lard
salt

SAUCE
4 dried pasilla chillies
4 dried mulato chillies
8 dried ancho chillies
2 tomatoes, halved
1/2 cup vegetable oil
2 tbsp sesame seeds
2 tbsp peanuts
2 tbsp almonds, chopped
1 onion, sliced
2 cloves garlic, chopped
2 tbsp raisins
1 ripe cooking banana,
chopped
1 whole clove
2.5cm (1in) piece
cinnamon
2 tsp dried oregano
2 tsp dried thyme
1/2 tsp aniseed
2 tbsp lard
50g (2oz) tablet mexican
drinking chocolate,
chopped
1 quantity shredded
chicken (page 133), plus
broth
1 packet dried corn
husks or banana leaves

TAMALES DE MOLE NEGRO OAXAQUENO
[steamed corn cakes filled with oaxacan black sauce]

Tamales are made from freshly ground white corn that has been boiled with slaked lime then ground and made into dough. The dough is wrapped in a corn husk, stuffed with filling, and steamed until light and fluffy. When prepared correctly, **tamales** are one of the most delicious snacks I've ever come across. The variations are limited only by the cook's imagination — try it with any of the fillings from the previous recipes. The filling I have included here is the most famous mole *(sauce)* from the state of Oaxaca. In the marketplace in Centro de Abastos, these **tamales** hold pride of place — and rightly so. Somewhere between a stew and a thick sauce, it can also be served separately with rice and a salad.

to make the dough, tip the boiling water into a mixing bowl and pour in the semolina in a slow, steady stream, stirring constantly. let stand for 15 minutes. combine the *masa harina* with the baking powder, then mix it with the semolina and stir through the lard. add salt to taste, cover and allow to cool.

meanwhile, make the sauce. dry-fry the chillies in a heavy-based frying pan until they are almost black (but don't burn them), then soak in cold water for 30 minutes. place the tomatoes cut-side down on a sheet of aluminium foil and roast under a very hot grill for 15 minutes. reserve the juices. peel off the blackened skin and discard. place the tomato flesh and juice in a food processor or blender.

heat a little of the vegetable oil in the frying pan and fry the sesame seeds until golden, then put them in the food processor or blender. do the same with the peanuts and almonds.

heat a little more oil in the pan and fry the onion and garlic until soft. stir in the raisins and cook for 1 minute. add the onion mixture to the food processor or blender, along with the banana, herbs and spices. drain the chillies, add them to the mixture and puree until the sauce is very smooth, moistening with a little water as necessary.

heat the lard and fry the pureed mixture over medium heat for 20 minutes, taking care that it doesn't catch on the bottom of the pan. add the chocolate and 1 cup chicken broth, and continue cooking for 30 minutes, or until the sauce coats the back of a spoon. remove from heat, stir in the shredded chicken and allow to cool.

to assemble the **tamales**, simmer 12 corn husks (or banana leaves, if using) in water for 10–15 minutes, or until pliable. drain and shake off excess water. lay the husks flat and put about 3 tablespoons dough in the centre of each. spread the dough into a rectangle, leaving a 3–4cm ($1^1/_4$–$1^1/_2$) border. spoon a generous amount of the filling into the centre of the dough. fold in the two long sides so they overlap, then fold in one of the short sides (leaving one side open allows the dough to expand). loosely tie each tamale parcel with a piece of string or a strip of corn husk.

place a collapsible vegetable steamer in a deep saucepan and pour in water until it just reaches the bottom of the steamer. stack the **tamales** with the open end facing up and steam for 1–$1^1/_2$ hours, adding more water if necessary. the **tamales** are done when the husk peels away easily. allow to cool for 5 minutes, then serve.

glossary

allspice berries

(also known as *pimento* or *Jamaican pepper*) An aromatic pepper related to the myrtle tree. The dried berries are used sparingly, either whole or crushed, primarily to enhance the fragrance of a dish.

asafoetida

A resin from the plant *fenula asafoetadia*, which is grown in Afghanistan and Iran. It has quite an unpleasant aroma, but imparts a subtle flavour when cooked. It is used in very small quantities in Indian cuisine, primarily to prevent flatulence. However, strict followers of Krishna philosophy are forbidden to consume garlic and onion, so devotees use asafoetida as a substitute seasoning. Those whose religious beliefs are less strict tend to indulge their tastebuds by using garlic, onion and asafoetida. Available from Asian food stores.

atta

(also known as *chapati flour*) A very fine, soft-textured wholemeal flour with a low gluten content — ideal for hand-kneaded Indian breads. Available from Asian food stores.

besan

(also known as *chickpea flour*) Predominantly used in Indian cooking, besan is made from ground chickpeas. It has a distinctive, nutty flavour, and is used to thicken batter or mixed with plain flour to make pastry. Available from Asian food stores.

betel leaves

Occasionally used in Southeast Asian cooking to wrap food before grilling on a barbecue. When grilled or steamed, betel leaves impart a subtle, tart, citric flavour. If unavailable, substitute foil.

burghul

Cracked wheat, predominantly used in the Middle East, where it is a main ingredient in tabouleh, kibbeh and felafels. Available from supermarkets, health food stores and Middle Eastern food stores.

candlenut

A tough, slightly bitter and oily nut, used ground in pastes as a thickening agent for curries, soups and stews. Its oil has been used as lamp fuel, hence its English name. Available from Asian food stores. If unavailable, substitute ground blanched almonds.

chao shao

Chinese roast pork. Basted with hoi sin sauce, the pork is roasted free-standing in an oven for what seems an eternity. The result is a glazed skin, deep red in colour, with a succulent, strong flavour. Ideal for stir-fries, or served or served on its own on a bed of plain rice.

chillies

Debate rages about which chillies are the hottest (the Thai's refer to their favourite birdseye chilli as the 'devil's penis') and from what part of the chilli the heat emanates. However, I've always found one rule to be true — a hot chilli is a hot chilli, no matter which part you consume. In most instances, I have tried to stay as close to the original concept of a dish as possible, but if you don't like the heat of chillies, feel free to reduce the amount or eliminate them from the dish altogether.

Does chilli have a flavour of it's own? Absolutely. There are numerous varieties of chillies, many of which have their own distinctive flavour. The Mexicans have an infinite number of *moles* (sauces) and salsas that depend on their wealth of various chillies. Yet chillies have other benefits as well: they increase the body's metabolic rate, which in turn stimulates the appetite and aids digestion.

Small specks of red or green chilli in a dish can really add to its visual appeal, and if it is this aspect that is most sought after, there is no doubt that seeding and scraping the inside of the chilli — always under cold running water — greatly curbs its prowess.

ancho chilli: A dried chilli, deep mahogany in colour, with a mild, sweet flavour. Used in Mexican cooking, it is ideal for chilli pastes, salsas and *moles* (sauces).

banana chilli: A large, yellow, mild to medium-hot chilli. Somewhere between a pepper (capsicum) and a chilli in flavour, it is ideal for salads, salsas and stews.

birdseye chilli: Small yet fiery, the birdseye chilli is bright red in colour and available both fresh and dried. It is the most commonly used chilli in Southeast Asia, and is nicknamed 'devil's penis' in Thailand.

chipotle chilli: A smoked and dried red jalapeño, which is added to moles (sauces) and salsas in Mexican cooking to impart a smoky flavour.

jalapeño chilli: A very hot, medium to dark green chilli, about 8–10cm (3–4in) in length. Used extensively in Mexican salsas, jalapeño chillies can be purchased in cans or bottles and are available at most supermarkets.

mulato chilli: A dark reddish-brown dried chilli, similar in appearance to the ancho, though slightly larger. It has an intense, smoky flavour and is excellent in mole-style sauces and fresh salsas.

pasilla chilli: A long, shiny block or graphite grey dried chilli with a pungent, earthy flavour. Used as a base for the Oaxacan black mole, it also goes extremely well with all seafood.

serrano chilli: A cigar-shaped, bright green to bright red chilli. Its piquant bite is well suited to fresh salsas. It can also be used dried or roasted in sauces.

chorizo

A spicy pork sausage of Spanish origin, made with plenty of garlic.

coconut milk

Used extensively in Southeast Asian and Indian cooking to thicken and balance the heat of various spices. The traditional method for making coconut milk involves shredding the white coconut flesh and soaking it in water for several hours. The swollen pulp is then placed in a muslin cloth and squeezed to extract the liquid, which is quite thick (coconut cream). This process is repeated, giving a thinner liquid (coconut milk). For the sake of convenience, used canned coconut milk. The fact is, wherever one finds the canned alternative, be it at a local delicatessen or a village market at the foothills of the Himalaya, it is an option both street hawker and home cook share.

coriander

(fresh coriander is also known as *cilantro* or *Chinese parsley*) Fresh coriander is one of the most fragrant and flavoursome of all herbs. It has a bright green, flat leaf and a long stem, and is sometimes sold in bunches with the root still attached. The roots or stems are usually finely chopped and added during cooking, while the leaves are more suitable as a garnish or are stirred into the dish at the end of cooking.

Coriander seeds are dry-roasted and ground to produce a spice which is an essential ingredient in a multitude of curry pastes, spice mixes and sauces.

curry leaves

Used fresh or dried, curry leaves are an essential addition to many curry pastes, and are often tossed into a stock or stew in much the same way bay leaves are used in western cooking. Fresh and dried leaves are available from most specialty grocers.

dhal

Used extensively in Indian cooking, dhal are lentils, which come in many varieties. *Toor dhal* (also known as *arhar dhal*) are red lentils, *urad dhal* are black husked lentils, and *channa dhal* are yellow split chickpeas.

dried shrimp

An ingredient in many Southeast Asian dishes, dried shrimp have an intense flavour. They are ground and added to soups and pastes, or soaked and added to stir-fries. Available from Asian food stores.

fish sauce

(also known as *nam pla*) Used throughout Southeast Asia, fish sauce is made from fermented small fish or prawns (shrimp). It is salty with a uniquely pungent aroma, though it mellows when combined with other ingredients.

galangal

A bulbous root that is used in Southeast Asian cuisine either freshly sliced or dried and ground. Galangal is similar to ginger, but with a more subtle flavour. It is used extensively in Thai cooking to add flavour to soups and curries, and to balance the rich and sweet. Available from specialty grocers and Asian food stores.

ikan bilis

Small dried anchovies, used in Malaysian and Indonesian sambals and as a flavour-booster in stocks. Available from Asian food stores.

kaffir lime leaves

Small, dark, shiny green leaves essential to Thai curries and soups. The sharp fragrance cuts the richness of coconut and bolsters all the flavours of a simple soup. The dried leaves are widely available, but fresh leaves are preferable. When you buy fresh leaves, keep them in the freezer, wrapped in a plastic bag. You can then use a few leaves when needed and continue to have a fresh supply on hand. Both fresh and dried kaffir lime leaves are available from most Asian grocery stores.

kecap manis

A cloyingly sweet, thickened soy sauce, used only in Indonesian cooking.

lemon grass

Fragrant, with overtones of citrus, lemon grass is a long green stalk with a white/cream, bulbous base. Only the bottom 10–12cm (4–5in) is used, either ground in curry pastes or sliced and added to sauces and stocks. Fresh lemon grass is widely available; it can also be purchased in jars or dried.

143

masa harina　　A very fine flour mode from ground corn kernels, traditionally used to make tortillas.

mustard seeds　　Black, brown or yellow, mustard seeds are used in Indian cooking to add a certain punch to curries, dhal dishes and condiments. They must first be fried until they 'pop' to release their flavour. There seems to be no hard and fast rule as to which seed is used and where — appearance seems to play a large role.

noodles　　One rule is supreme when preparing noodles — fresh is best. When using fresh noodles, the trick is to rinse well and add right at the end of cooking. With the dried variety, some soaking or cooking is usually required, so it's best to follow packet directions.

Particular care must be taken in the choice of noodles: for example, fine 'glass' noodles add a luscious finesse to a Thai salad, yet are too fragile for stir-fries; overcooked rice noodles can disintegrate and release a slimy starch that will spoil a dish. As with all food, cooking does not stop once the dish is removed from the source of heat, so when testing noodles for 'doneness', remove them from the heat when they are almost cooked through.

glass noodles: (also known as *bean thread noodles, cellophane noodles* or *green bean vermicelli*) Glass noodles become transparent when cooked, and are more often used in soups than in stir-fries. They are sold in bundles.

hokkien noodles: Bright yellow in colour, hokkien noodles are thick egg noodles which resemble spaghetti. They are ideal for both soups and stir-fries. Available fresh from many supermarkets and most Asian food stores.

rice noodles: Made from rice flour, rice noodles are opaque and are excellent for stir-fries.

oils　　Although I have not always specified which type of oil to use for the recipes in this book, it is worthwhile to be aware of the suitability of certain oils for certain dishes. Some oils are best for frying, other for dressing, and others still for their aromatic qualities.

olive oil: For a rich, full-flavoured oil, it is hard to surpass extra virgin cold-pressed olive oil. This is best used in dressings over hot or cold foods, and when frying at low temperatures. A more subtle flavour is achieved by using 'light' olive oil.

peanut oil: An excellent oil for stir-fries or deep frying, because of its ability to handle high temperatures without breaking up. Not recommended for use in dishes that are cooked at low temperatures, or in dressings. Corn oil is the next best choice or, for a healthier alternative, try safflower or sunflower oil or a blended vegetable oil.

sesame oil: A highly aromatic oil, predominantly used in Asian cuisines. Sesame oil has a very strong flavour, so should be used sparingly as an aromatic garnish, or in conjunction with a good-quality frying oil. Not recommended for use at prolonged high temperatures.

orange water	Distilled from bitter oranges, orange water is used as a flavouring in many Middle Eastern dishes.
palm sugar	(also known as *jaggery*) A sandy to dark-brown sugar obtained from the palmyrah palm, palm sugar has a unique taste. Extensively used in Southeast Asian cooking as an ingredient in both savoury and sweet dishes. Available from Asian food stores.
pandanus leaves	Used in Southeast Asian cooking to add a distinctive 'woody flavour' to a dish. Pandanus leaves are also used to wrap food, particularly rice, which is then steamed or barbecued. Fresh pandanus leaves are preferable, but frozen will suffice. Available from Asian food stores. If unavailable, substitute foil.
pea eggplants	Flavour-absorbing, pea-sized pods with a slightly tart flavour, popular in Thai curries and soups. Available from specialty grocers. If unavailable, use standard eggplant.
pomelo	Similar to grapefruit, but usually larger, with a very thick peel. The flesh can be yellow, pink or orange and is quite sweet.
queso fresco	(literally, 'fresh cheese') A very mild white cheese, used in Mexican cooking. *Queso fresco* is difficult to find outside Mexico, so substitute Italian-style fresh mozzarella or bocconcini — even a mild cheddar will do.
rice	**basmati rice:** A fragrant long grain rice cultivated in India and Pakistan. Basmati holds its shape and texture long after other types of rice would have turned to mush. Great for pilaf, biriyani (Indian-style fried rice) and served plain with curries.

black rice: A highly glutinous, purple-black short grain rice that is prepared in Southeast Asia almost exclusively as a sweet. If unavailable, substitute white glutinous rice.

jasmine rice: A long grain, white and beautifully perfumed rice that is essential to the Thai experience. Ideal for gentle steaming and served plain.

sticky rice: Either a pearly-white or purple/black rice which becomes glutinous when cooked, and is combined with coconut cream and fruit and used for sweets such as **klaow niaow mamuang** (mango with sticky rice) on page 62. Alternatively, there is a savoury sticky rice, still much preferred by the farmers and peasants in the north of Thailand where it is hand-rolled into balls, dipped in a sauce and eaten with the hands as described on page 54. |
ice wine	A sweet wine made from fermented rice. Available from Asian food stores.
ice wine vinegar	A vinegar distilled from fermented rice, used in dressings and sauces. Available from Asian food stores.
gani	Wild Greek marjoram. This herb is not widely available, but marjoram or oregano can be substituted successfully.

rosewater

An essence distilled by steaming rose petals. Although quite expensive, only very little is needed to perfume a sweet into the aromatic heavens. Can be substituted with rose essence or concentrate.

sambal olek

Crushed fresh chillies in vinegar, flavoured with garlic, ginger, salt and sugar. Used sparingly in many Indonesian and Malaysian dishes — beware of its tongue-numbing heat. Most supermarkets now carry a chilli paste of some description that will suffice, but it's best to make your own and store it in the refrigerator.

To make sambal olek, grind a handful of chopped fresh red chillies with 2 cloves garlic and 1 teaspoon salt in a mortar and pestle. Transfer to a jar and add a 2.5cm (1in) piece of ginger, finely julienned, and 1 teaspoon sugar. Mix well to combine. Drizzle a thin layer of vegetable oil over the top. Store in the refrigerator for a few weeks before using, to allow the flavours to develop.

sambar powder

A spice mix used to make the South Indian vegetable dish *sambar*. Variations are endless, but most sambar powders are a combination of coriander seeds, cumin, fenugreek seeds, mustard seeds, cinnamon, turmeric and ground lentils. The spices are then dry-roasted or fried immediately prior to adding the vegetables and liquids. Available from specialist spice stores and Indian food stores.

semolina

Sifted from durum wheat or from regular wheat, semolina is sold in coarse, medium and fine grades. Used in savoury and sweet dishes, it adds a lightness to cakes, breads and biscuits when used in conjunction with plain flour.

shredded coconut

Grated then dried coconut flesh, available in packets from Asian food stores and most supermarkets.

To toast shredded coconut, spread the required amount on a baking tray and place under a griller or in an oven set on low. Alternatively, toast in an unoiled wok over low heat, shaking the wok occasionally to make sure the coconut toasts evenly. No matter which method you use, watch the coconut carefully — it should only take a minute or two before it is ready.

shrimp paste

(also known as *blachan*) A pungent, smooth paste made from dried prawns, shrimp paste is sold in small cans and, once opened, keeps well in the refrigerator. Use sparingly as its flavour is intense.

To grill shrimp paste, spread the required amount on a strip of aluminium foil and place under a hot griller for about 1 minute or until it begins to bubble. Alternatively, cook in a frying pan with a little oil for about 1 minute until fragrant, breaking it up with a fork as it cooks.

sweet chilli sauce

This is to Thailand's street vendor what tomato sauce or ketchup is to the purveyor of the hot dog. Sweet chilli sauce is made from crushed chillies, sugar syrup, vinegar, salt and, at times, garlic, shrimp paste and/or fish sauce. Available from most supermarkets and Asian food stores — look for a brand that has been imported from Thailand.

tahini

A thick paste made from sesame seeds, used in Middle Eastern cooking. Available from health food stores and supermarkets.

tamarind

A leguminous tree from India with pods that contain a black-brown acidic pulp and seed. The pulp is used to make tamarind water, which is added during cooking to cut richness and lift the flavour of soups, curries, chutneys and even ice-cream. The packaged pulp is available form Asian food stores, and is far superior to pre-prepared tamarind paste.

To make 1 cup tamarind water, soak 60g (2oz) tamarind pulp in 1 cup boiling water and allow to steep for 15 minutes. When the water has cooled, use your fingers to strip the pulp from the seeds to help it dissolve. Strain the mixture, reserving the liquid and discarding the seeds and fibres. Use tamarind water in the quantities indicated in a recipe.

tempeh

A fermented soya bean 'cake', mustard yellow in colour, popular all over Indonesia. It has a strong, smoky flavour that many visitors to Indonesia find unpalatable. Usually served sliced and deep-fried until golden and crunchy.

thai basil

There are actually three types of basil the Thais use depending on the nature of the dish. Thai basil has a powerful anise perfume and flavour and is used predominantly in green and red curries. Lemon basil is used in soups and imparts a wonderful aroma. Holy basil has leaves with deep purple hearts and a clove-like aftertaste, and is used in stir-fries and salads. All are available from Asian or specialty grocers.

tomatillos

(also known as *Mexican green tomatoes* or *husk tomatoes*) When ripe, these tomatoes remain green and firm, with a slightly acidic flavour. They are particularly good in Mexican-style salsas. Available from some specialty suppliers. If unavailable, substitute firm red tomatoes.

vietnamese mint

An attractive herb with green and purple leaves, and an aroma somewhere between basil and mint with aniseed overtones. Used as a garnish in curries and soups, or tossed into a stir-fry at the end of cooking. Available from specialty grocers.

acknowledgments

There would be no book without all the people whose food I've shared, whose homes I've entered, whose patience I've tested and whose names I've forgotten — for the constant traveller the personal embrace is sorrowfully short and intensely sweet.

Of the people I wish to thank whose names I *can* remember, first and foremost are my wonderfully supportive parents, who not only encouraged me to explore other cultures but to do something with the knowledge and experience garnered — I hope I have done some justice to all those times when you hadn't the slightest clue where I was. Thanks also to my brother and sister who, as willing guineapigs and enthusiastic taste-testers, helped to bring the wild experimentations into line.

Most importantly, I would like to thank all my co-travellers, those masochistic lovers of life who have put up with my travelling personas, wild mood swings and eccentric requests. In particular to the wit, wisdom and infectious exuberance of James Compton, who taught me the beauty of voyeurism and how to get fat in India. Also to Raymond, Suza, Libba and the countless others with whom I shared some very special stolen moments, now frozen in time.

Special thanks to the patience and resolve of Tamara Da Silva, who not only encouraged me but provided house and home while completing this book. She bore my frustrations and aberrant moods and knew when it was necessary to use the stockwhip to good effect.

Many thanks also to Jacqui Triggs, who not only showed me the way around a computer but how to kick and abuse it when human incompetence stepped in. And to those cuckoo cooks with whom I've shared many a kitchen, Tim and Tony. Don't forget, we know where those white coats really come from.

A mention must also go to the pioneers of backpacking, the irreplaceable guidebooks and, in particular, the Lonely Planet series, which held my hand through much of the solo journeying.